EAR TRAINING and SIGHT SINGING

Also by Maurice Lieberman

ELEMENTARY KEYBOARD HARMONY

EAR TRAINING

AND

SIGHT SINGING

MAURICE LIEBERMAN

W · W · NORTON & COMPANY

New York · London

TO OUR TWO WONDERFUL YOUNG PEOPLE,

Shelly and Peter

W. W. Norton & Company, Inc., 500 Fifth Avenue, New York, N.Y. 10110
W. W. Norton & Company Ltd., 10 Coptic Street, London, WC1A 1PU

Library of Congress Catalog Card No. 59-6083

Music autographed by Maxwell Weaner

ISBN 0-393-09519-3

PRINTED IN THE UNITED STATES OF AMERICA

3 4 5 6 7 8 9 0

CONTENTS

Entries in roman type indicate rhythm study. *Entries in italic type indicate tonal study.* Sight-singing melodies include both rhythm and tonal material.

PREFACE

EXPERIENCED teachers of ear training and sight singing realize that in this area the student's progress depends on skillful guidance, encouragement, and a reasonably good text.

Ear Training and Sight Singing is the result of years of experimentation in this field; it is a tool to help the development of the skills a student must have. Comprehensive in scope and easily understandable, it offers close to a thousand carefully selected melodies and rhythm exercises. In addition, there are numerous exercises in tonal and rhythmic drill, intervals, memorization, analysis, modulation, and so on. The resultant skills are synthesized at each level of advancement in melodies selected from the literature and folk song which are both germane to the problems and free of irrelevant factors.

Tonal study is centered on the attainment of a sure sense of relative pitch, so that the student learns to sing major, minor, and modulatory melodies with ease. Interval practice proceeds simultaneously to enable the student to cope with remote modulations and nontonal melody. Students should therefore be required to practice intervals as well as the tonal studies daily. These scale and chord tone groups inculcate a feeling of "pitch distance" from the tonic and tonic chord tones. Teachers who favor the *sol-fa* syllables should require students to translate the numbers into syllables. Unencumbered by notation, the tone groups serve to center attention on tones relative to the tonic, which are then correlated to written symbols. The teacher may write different scales on the blackboard, and then point to various notes for the students to sing. Melodies should be assigned for rapid recitation by scale step number (or syllable) without singing the notes, to assure unhesitating identification of any note in any key. The first five Sections, some three hundred melodies, are exclusively in major and minor. Interval practice includes singing and letter naming every interval, up and down from a given series of notes.

Modulation to closely related keys can also be sung by means of relative pitch. Modulatory melodies in Sections 6, 7, and 8 are provided with dual identification clues to key changes. These clues alert the student to the manner in which such modulations are made melodically, and he is then better prepared to discover such modulations in melodies without marked clues.

The rhythm exercises depart from the customary practice of moving almost directly to the split beat. Instead, these studies commence with the whole beat, then move on to two-, three-, and four-beat values. The student thus obtains a solid grasp of duration proportions which apply readily to fractions of a beat. Compound meter is postponed until the student has mastered the single-beat triplet in simple meter, which is then related to the superbeat in compound meter. Similarly the duplet, superbeat, and quadruplet

ix

in compound meter are treated jointly with the same divisions of the beat in simple meter.

Chordal study is limited to the knowledge required for an understanding of chord-line skips and modulation. Reading the tenor clef is delayed until the alto clef has been mastered.

The teacher should be able to devote the major part of class sessions to drill, sight-singing, and dictation, since the text furnishes the rudiments of music, scale, interval and chord structure, notation, key signatures, repetition signs, clef notation, and elementary form. Charts of the piano keyboard, relative minor and near-related keys, the modes and enharmonic intervals are also included, as well as a series of exercises for home practice in singing and writing. The teacher will find that the material, with Chapter 8 as the dividing point, can be covered in two semesters, depending on the general level of the class and the frequency of class sessions.

                                                                M. L.

CHAPTER

1

Rhythm

THE basic elements of music are tone and time. These elements used without purpose, design, or feeling do not constitute music. The sound of aimless banging on a drum or the wail of a siren is not music. Tones and time, when *organized* in patterns, become the materials of music, irrespective of whether the patterns are obvious or subtle, conventional or novel. Organized time becomes rhythm and patterned tones in rhythm become melody and harmony.

Rhythm, a word derived from the Greek, meaning "the flow of measured motion," implies in a broad sense the flow of movement felt in the sweep of the lines in poetry, in the procession of episodes in a drama, or in the successive sections of a musical work, which imparts in each instance a sense of balance to the over-all pattern. By extension, the term *rhythm* is also applied to the feeling of movement in space. We speak of the "rhythm" of the Parthenon's portico, meaning the impression received of regular motion as the eye, in a sweeping glance, catches each column at regular intervals. Patterns of line, mass, and color in a painting similarly impart a feeling of rhythm.

On a different and more tangible level, the term rhythm describes repeated patterns of physical movement, as in dancing and physical labor. Dancing, marching, and work motions, both regular and irregular, are reflected in the time element, or rhythm, of music. Conversely the rhythms in dance and marching music have the power to induce physical movement "in time" with the music. We tend to move, sway, or respond with an inner muscular tension and relaxation when watching people engaged in rhythmic action and when listening to music with strong rhythmic characteristics. Such responses extend to regular motion in nature—the rhythmic crash of the surf or trees swaying in the wind— and even to the rhythmic sound of machinery in motion. Our response to physical and musical rhythm undoubtedly reflects an awareness of some of the rhythms of our being—the muscular tension and relaxation in walking, running, breathing; the beating of the heart; and other involuntary or instinctive rhythmic motion.

Regular motion like walking provides one type of rhythm. Single patterns of dance or work motion which are repeated set up a different type of rhythm. These small patterns have their counterparts in small musical time patterns called *rhythmic figures*. A rhythmic figure may be com-

pared with the dot-dash rhythm of a single letter in Morse code. The
term *rhythm* is also applied to the time relationship of two or more tones
anywhere in a piece of music. All of these aspects of rhythm are present
in a musical work, like embroidered patterns on the folds of a large
drapery.

Rhythm is a means of expressing feeling. Just as a fast or slow stride,
regular or irregular motion, may reflect states of mind and feeling, so
corresponding rhythms may express emotion of one kind or another.
Rhythm also has its source in a basic human desire to find or create order
in nature and in our environment—mankind's need to identify, classify,
and measure everything, including time.

Our first study deals with relations in time as applied to music. A clock
measures time by ticking at uniformly established intervals called seconds.
Comparable to this is the evenly-spaced stroke of the bass drummer in a
military parade. Such regularly-spaced strokes are called *beats* or *pulsa-
tions*, musical terms which reflect the regularity of heart and pulse action.
Unlike clock seconds, drum beats may be stroked at a uniformly faster
or slower rate. The rate of the beats is called the *tempo*. The tempo of
the beats in Fig. 1b is faster than in 1a; the tempo in Fig. 1c is slower
than in 1a.

Fig. 1

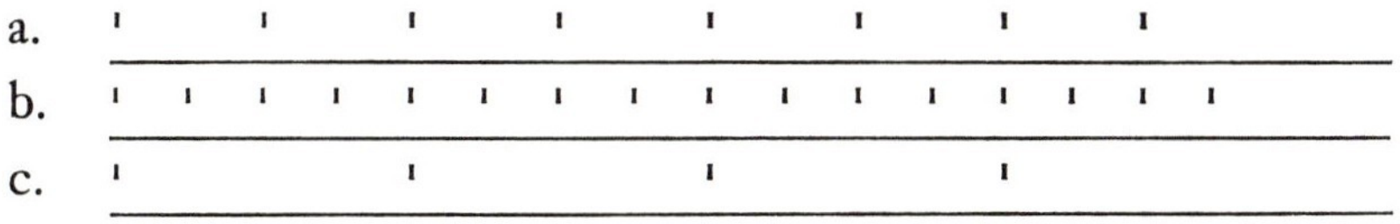

In terms of clock time, the slow beats in Fig. 1c may be sounded as
far as a second apart; those in Fig. 1b may come rapidly at quarter-second
intervals. Fast tempos in music may give rise to feelings of excitement,
vivacity, or turbulence; slow tempos are often associated with peace,
calm, introspection, weariness, or grief.

You may have noticed that a bass-drum player alternates a heavy
downstroke with a lighter upstroke. He may also beat on alternate strides.
In doing so, he is following a natural tendency to group beats by twos.
This tendency exhibits itself even when no regular stress is present. The
sound of a clock ticking becomes TICK-tick, TICK-tick in our minds;
an even marching step becomes LEFT-right, LEFT-right. Grouping
beats by accenting every other or every third beat is a musical way of
dividing a stream of beats, as shown in Fig. 1, into a continuous series of
two-beat or three-beat groups. Figs. 2a and 2b show how this is done;
the sign > means accent.

Fig. 2

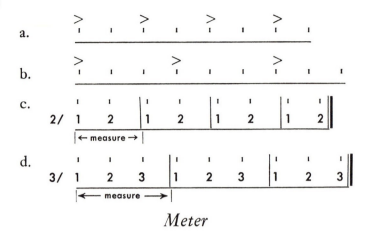

Meter

The patterns into which a stream of beats may be divided are called meters, from the Greek *metreo*, to measure. Each beat group starts on the normally accented beat—this is indicated in written music by a short vertical line called the *bar line*—and ends with the next bar line. The bar lines divide the stream of beats into *measures*, each of which contains one primary accent and one or more afterbeats. The measure is thus the time interval from one primary accent to the next, as is shown in Figs. 2c and 2d. Musicians may sometimes refer to a given measure as, say, the "fifth bar."

The last bar line in a composition is written with a light and a heavy line, and is called a *double bar;* one is shown in Fig. 2c. The very first bar line, beat one of measure one, is omitted. When a composition is divided into two or more sections, a light double bar separates the sections.

Two beats in a measure—one accented and one unaccented—is called *simple duple meter;* three beats in a measure—one accented and two unaccented afterbeats—is called *simple triple meter.* Simple duple and triple meters are the basic ways to organize beats.

The composer indicates the meter at the beginning of a composition by a fraction, the *meter signature* (usually referred to as a *time signature*). The numerator of this fraction indicates the number of beats to a measure, as illustrated in Figs. 2c and 2d. In most compositions the same meter is used from beginning to end, although changes in meter occur in some types of folk music and in contemporary music (see Fig. 5f).

Duple meter is frequently used for vigorous music, as in marches; triple meter is often employed for tender or graceful music, as in the waltz. Both march and dance music, with few exceptions, are characterized by strongly marked first beats. Compositions which project a quiet or contemplative mood do not have strongly accented first beats; mood, melodic contour, and rhythm pattern may require the suppression of the metric accent. Music in simple duple and triple meter, as we will see, may also have characteristic *off accents*.

Two units of duple meter joined form *simple quadruple meter*, as shown in Fig. 3; the first-beat accent is followed by a lighter accent on beat three.

Fig. 3

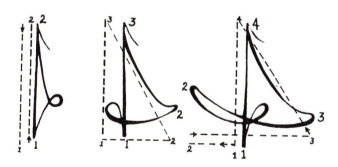

Choral and orchestral conductors are primarily concerned with rendering a composition according to the composer's intentions. They must, among other things, set the tempo, alter it when necessary, and beat the

Fig. 4

meter of a work from start to finish. Diagrams illustrating the conductor's beat in simple meter are drawn in unbroken lines in Fig. 4. The broken-line diagrams are the same movements simplified. The direction of the beats as given in Fig. 4 is standard, although variations on these beat-motions are used by different conductors. Note that the duple-meter beat resembles the strokes of the bass drummer. Practice beating simple meters using the motions of Fig. 4.

Dance music and march music require a steady tempo from start to finish (Fig. 5a). A more pliable beat is generally necessary in music with expressive meaning. Tempo may be varied by gradually hastening the beats; the direction to do this is given by the word *accelerando* written under or within the measure (Fig. 5b). The beats may be slowed up gradually, which is indicated by the word *ritardando* (Fig. 5c). One beat may be held back, and then the tempo resumed by quickly catching up on the next beat, the direction to do this is the word *rubato* (Fig. 5d).

Or a beat may be held for double or more than double its normal length; the beat to be so held has a *fermata*, ⌢, written over it (Fig. 5e). The student should refer to the Glossary, p. 326, for the meaning of tempo and expression terms used in the music in this book.

Fig. 5

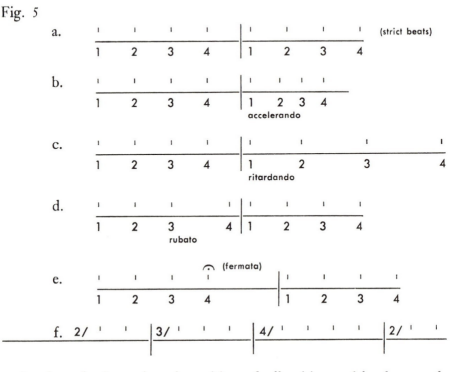

Accelerandos in conjunction with gradually rising and louder sounds create mounting excitement and tension. Conversely, ritardandos accompanied by gradually falling and diminishing sounds produce the sensation of moving from tension or climax to a plateau of resolution. Rubatos —literally "robbing" a beat, by giving more time to the preceding beat— may be compared to two people walking in step together. One falls behind for a step, and then catches up. Rubatos are seldom indicated in music, but are left to the taste and judgment of the performer. The fermata is most frequently found at the end of a composition or at end of a section, although it is also used within music to indicate that one particular tone should be held.

The Beat Unit and the Metric Signature

We indicated single beats in Figs. 1-3 by a series of dots. In music, beats are represented by note symbols, any one of which may denote one beat. These same symbols may also have more or less than the duration value of a single beat, but for the present we need only recognize that any one of them may be used to represent a single beat. They are *time* symbols, and do not represent any particular sound, high or low, until they are placed on a music staff.

These one-beat symbols are: *whole note,* ○; *half note,* ♩; *quarter note,* ♩; *eighth note,* ♪; *sixteenth note,* ♬. Observe that the half note looks like the whole note with a *stem* at its side. The stem of this and other notes may be drawn down: ♩ , in which case the stem is placed on the left side of the notehead. The quarter note looks like the half with the notehead filled in; the eighth note looks like the quarter with a *hook* or *flag* at the end of its stem. When two or more eighth notes are used in succession, a *beam* connecting the stems is substituted for the flags: ♫♫ . Flags are retained in vocal music when separate notes are required for separate syllables of the text. Sixteenth notes look like eighths with double flags or double beams: ♬♬, ♬♬ ; sixteenth-note beams are run under eighth-note beams. Beams, with rare exception, are not drawn across the bar line. Practice writing these notes.

When any of these notes is used to represent a single beat, that symbol is called the *beat unit.* Thus, /○ = one beat; /♩ = one beat; /♩ = one beat; /♪ = one beat; /♬ = one beat. The composer may use any of these symbols to represent one beat. The reasons for his choice of one or another beat unit will be explained later.

The simple meters, shown above in Figs. 2c and 2d, and Fig. 3, may thus be written in *any* of the following ways (Fig. 6):

Fig. 6

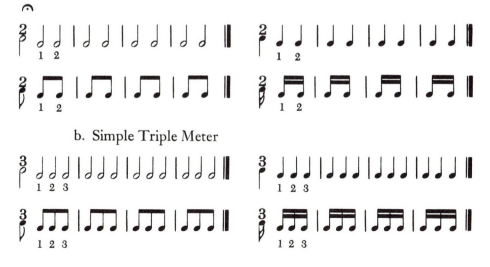

a. Simple Duple Meter

b. Simple Triple Meter

c. Simple Quadruple Meter

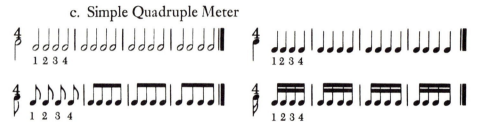

The combined meter and beat-unit symbols in Fig. 6 are written so in order to clarify the meaning of meter signature. Composers write 2/♩ as 2/2; 3/♩ as 3/4; 4/♪ as 4/8; and 4/♬ as 4/16. The numerator of these fractions indicates the number of beats in each measure; the denominator indicates which note-symbol is to be used as the single beat unit.

Rests

A silence may occur on any beat, and is indicated by a symbol called a *rest*. The rest in music has the same function as a pause in speech. We draw a breath at the end of a phrase and we subside in silence at the end of a sentence. We resort at times to short, clipped speech; we pause dramatically for effect. In music, rests separate segments of a melody or parts of a work. Or a series of short, clipped tones separated by short rests may be used. A long rest may precede the dramatic entrance of a solo part, the entrance of a group of instruments, the beginning of a new section, a new theme, or a different mood in a work.

Each of the following rest symbols may stand for silence on a single beat: The whole rest, ‒ , a rectangle hanging from a line (this symbol is rarely used as a single-beat rest); the half rest, ‒ , a rectangle resting on a line; a quarter rest, ᄼ , similar to the letter z written backward; the eighth rest, ᚈ , which looks somewhat like the number 7; and the sixteenth rest, ᚈ , which is like the eighth rest, but has two hooks. Practice writing the rest symbols. In some foreign editions, the eighth rest turned backward, ᚈ , serves as a quarter rest.

Fig. 7 shows single-beat rests in the simple meters.*

Fig. 7 a. Single-beat Rests in Simple Duple Meter

* For the present we will continue to write rests of two or more beats' duration as shown in Fig. 7. However, a simpler method, which will be used later in connection with two- and three-beat note symbols, is to use the whole rest for whole-measure rests, regardless of the number of beats in a measure. Two-measure rests are written as in Fig. 9a; rests longer than two measures are as shown in Fig. 9b:

b. Single-beat Rests in Simple Triple Meter

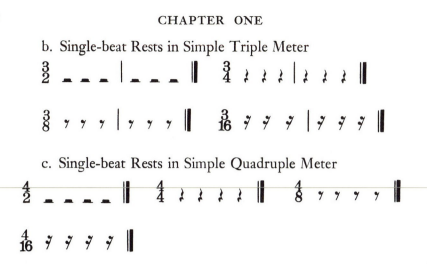

c. Single-beat Rests in Simple Quadruple Meter

Ex. 1a. The exercises in Fig. 8 on the use of single-beat notes and rests
are to be practiced like this: Clap one preliminary measure in slow,
even beats; two claps for duple meter, three for triple meter, four for
quadruple. Hold your hands apart on any beat with a rest.

Fig. 8

9.  [musical notation: $\frac{3}{16}$ time signature rhythm example]

Composite Meter

In some compositions the meter alternates: for example, 1 2 | 1 2 3 | 1 2 | 1 2 3, as in the second movement of Tchaikovsky's Symphony No. 6. The meter signature for this particular alternation is 5/4. Any combination of alternating simple meters forms a *composite meter*. Composite meters are named according to the number of beats which occur in any one measure. Thus, in Ex. 1b, lines one and two show *septuple meter;* line three is in *quintuple meter.* Quintuple meter may be made up of a group of 3 beats plus a group of 2, or 2 beats plus 3 beats. Septuple meter may be made up of a group of 3 beats plus a group of 4; of 4 plus 3; or a combination of groups of 2 beats and a group of three beats: 2 plus 2 plus 3; 3 plus 2 plus 2; or 2 plus 3 plus 2.

Ex. 1b.   Clap the rhythms in Fig. 10.

Fig. 10

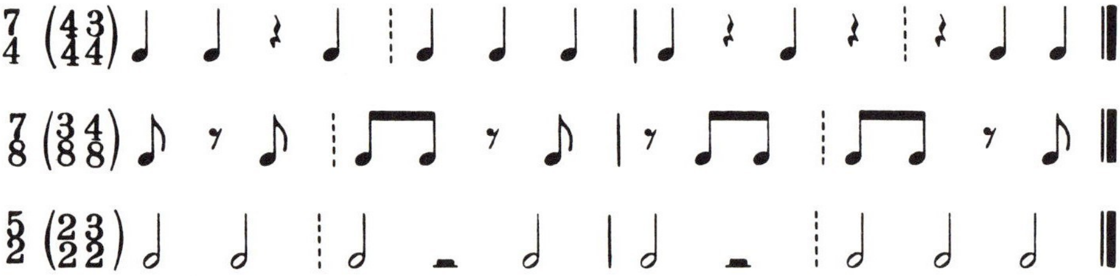

[musical notation: three rhythm lines in $\frac{7}{4}$ $(\frac{4}{4}\frac{3}{4})$, $\frac{7}{8}$ $(\frac{3}{8}\frac{4}{8})$, and $\frac{5}{2}$ $(\frac{2}{2}\frac{3}{2})$]

Dynamic Accent

In Fig. 2 the accented first beat, or metric accent, was marked by the symbol <. Accents used for expressive purposes may be placed on any beat, or as we shall see later, on any part of a beat. Expressive accents are called *dynamic accents.* Dynamic accents serve to reinforce the normally accented first-beat metric accent in march and dance music. Dynamic accents which occur regularly on unaccented or *offbeats* set up a rhythm called *syncopation:* *

[example: accent patterns on beats]

The displaced accents of syncopation conflict with the normal metric

* Other types of syncopated rhythms will be studied later in this book.

accents, and thus create rhythmic tension and excitement. The effect is heightened when rests fall on the metric accent, as in 2/4 ♪ ♪ | ♪ ♪; 3/4 ♪ ♪ ♪ | ♪ ♪ ♪; 4/4 ♪ ♪ ♪ ♪ | .

Ex. 1c.   In Fig. 11, tap the beats steadily with your foot while clapping the rhythm with a strong clap on the marked accents.

Fig. 11

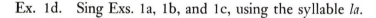

Ex. 1d.   Sing Exs. 1a, 1b, and 1c, using the syllable *la*.

Tempo and the Beat Unit

Turn back to Ex. 1a. Clap the beats in line 3 (4/2) at a fast tempo, then clap the beats in line 8 (4/8) at a slow tempo. The point of doing this is to see that half-note beat units are not necessarily slow beats, nor are eighth-note beat units necessarily fast. Bear this in mind: there are no notes which are *inherently* long or short. A note is long or short only in relation to tempo and in relation to other notes.

We may at present sum up these relations as follows: A note is long if it is a beat unit in a slow tempo, short if it is a beat unit in a fast tempo. A note is long if longer in duration than the beat unit value, short if it has less duration than the beat unit value. We will soon see that a tone can be held for longer than one beat, and also that a number of tones can be sung on a single beat. The composer's choice of a beat unit is often determined by this, since he will use that beat unit which makes it easy to read many tones on one beat.

So far in this book, whole, half, quarter, eighth, and sixteenth notes have been used as single-beat units. Tones may be prolonged to last for two or more beats by joining single-beat notes on the same tone with a curved line called a *tie*, thus: single beats, 2/4 ♩ ♩, two-beat value, 2/4 ♩ ♩. Single beats, 3/2 ♩ ♩ ♩, two-beat value, 3/2 ♩ ♩ ♩. Rests are not tied.

In vocal music, the second of the tied notes is not sung with a new breath; the tone is merely continued without a break for the added beat. On wind instruments, ties are played without taking a new breath. In piano performance, the finger holds the key down for the added beat; on the violin, the tied note is played without lifting the bow from the string. Tying applies only to the continuance of the same pitch. Two different pitches cannot be tied.

Ex. 2. Using a pencil, write two-beat ties into Fig. 8. Do not bind notes across the bar line. Now clap the revised rhythms, holding your palms together for two-beat notes. Sing these exercises with the syllable *la*, remembering that the second of these notes, the tied note, is not sung with a new breath.

A curved line over a series of tones, used in phrasing a melody, is called a *slur;* the slur encompasses all the tones which comprise a small melodic unit, such as a phrase, a half-phrase, or a motive. Notes covered by a slur should be sung smoothly, or *legato*. Dots over notes indicate that the tones should be short and detached; this kind of rendition is called *staccato*.

Notes as duration symbols have proportional values to each other. For instance, ♩ ♩ = 𝅝; ♩ ♩ = ♩; ♪ ♪ = ♩; and ♪ ♪ = ♪. The same relative values apply to rests: ▬ ▬ = ▬; 𝄽 𝄽 = ▬; 𝄾 𝄾 = 𝄽 ; and 𝄿 𝄿 = 𝄾 .

Therefore, when the beat is a ♩ and we wish to write a two-beat note, we may use 𝅝 instead of ♩ ♩. Other relationships may be outlined thus:

Beat unit	Two-beat value	Two-beat rest
♩	𝅝	▬
♩	♩	▬
♪	♩	𝄽
♪	♪	𝄾

Rhythmic figures like 4/16 𝅘𝅥𝅯𝅘𝅥𝅯, 4/8 ♩ ♫, 4/4 ♩ ♩ ♩, and 4/2 𝅝 ♩ ♩ are proportionately the same. The values are written differently in different meters. Compare 3/8 ♩ ♪, 3/4 ♩ ♩, and 3/2 𝅝 ♩

Ex. 3a. Tap even beats with your foot; then clap the rhythms in Fig. 12. Keep a steady beat and *keep your eyes on the measure ahead.* It is more important to grasp the rhythm of a *unit* of music—one or two measures, or still better, four measures—than the time values of single notes. If the beat drags or if you are forced to stop before the end of the line, you have taken too fast a tempo or you have failed to look ahead. Do not stretch the rests out for longer than their values.

Fig. 12

Sing these rhythms with *la*.

Many melodies commence with a preliminary beat before the first metric accent, for example, Flŏw | G̀ently Sweet Afton, and Th̆e | Ŏld Oaken Bucket. This preliminary beat is called an *upbeat** or *arsis*. Examine the diagrams in Fig. 4 again. You will see that the upbeat is indicated there by a preliminary upward swing before the arm comes down on the first metric accent, called the *downbeat* or *thesis*. The time value of an upbeat is subtracted from the final measure of a piece of music, so that a melody in 3/4 with a one-beat upbeat will have only two beats in its last measure.

Ex. 3b.   Clap the rhythms in Fig. 13, then sing each line with *la*. Note that when beams are divided, they follow the natural division in a measure: 4/8 ♫ ♫, not ♪ ♫♩. Also, the half rest is not used for two beats in 3/4 ♩▬ ; ♩ 𝄽𝄽 is clearer. In 3/8 ♪ 𝄾𝄾 is used, not ♪ 𝄽 .

* The term *upbeat* is also applied to preliminary fractions of a beat, and to a beat plus the fraction of a beat; these matters will be discussed below.

Fig. 13

Ex. 3c. Tap even beats with your foot, then clap four measures of the first line of Fig. 12. Look away from the page and write these measures down from memory. *Do not memorize single measures.* Try to feel the rhythm of the unit as a whole. Do not get discouraged by mistakes; your ability will develop with practice. Now memorize each half line of Exs. 3a and 3b.

CHAPTER

2

Characteristics of a Tone

THE basic elements of music, we have said, are time and tone. Musical sound—that is, tone—results when anything vibrates, be it a taut string, the air inside a tube, a drumhead, a bar or plate of wood or metal, or your vocal cords. These vibrations coming through the air are received by the ear and transmitted to the brain, which translates them as particular tones in accordance with its experiences and associations. A single tone, such as the *la* which you have used in rhythm practice, has four important characteristics: *duration, amplitude, timbre,* and *pitch*.

Duration of a tone is, of course, the length of time it is continuously produced or sounded. Amplitude, or volume, of a tone may be loud (indicated in music by the word *forte*, abbreviated f.), soft (*piano* , abbreviated *p.*), or lie anywhere between. Tonal volume may be increased gradually (indicated by *crescendo*, ============) or decreased gradually (*diminuendo*, ============). It may be suddenly decreased (indicated by *forte-piano*, abbreviated *fp.*), or suddenly increased (indicated by *accent, sforzando,* or *sforzato*, abbreviated *sfz., fz.*).

A tone's timbre is its distinctive quality, the characteristic that makes your *la* sound different from the same tone played on the oboe. Differences in timbre are due to differences in the prominence of *overtones* or *harmonics*. Overtones are faintly heard tones which sound with the tone being produced, the *fundamental* tone. A string or other medium which vibrates as a whole sounds a fundamental tone; but at the same time that the whole string is vibrating, segments of the string also vibrate and produce a series of higher and softer tones, the overtones.

Lastly, a tone has pitch, which may be defined as a steady level of sound. The pitch of a tone depends on the number of times per second the medium producing the sound is vibrating: the higher the number of vibrations per second, the higher the pitch of the tone produced. A pitch is fixed when the number of vibrations per second remains constant. The low growl of a fire-engine siren rising to a high piercing shriek is not a fixed pitch; the changing tone level is caused by gradually faster vibrations.

Intervals and Scales

On the piano, play any C and the next C above it together. They blend so perfectly that they sound like one tone. The reason for this is that the string which produces the upper C vibrates twice as fast as the string which produces the lower C. This 1:2 relationship between tones is called a *perfect octave*.

Whenever two tones are sounded, they produce an effect called an *interval*. Two tones sounded together form a *harmonic interval*. The same tones sounded in succession are called a *melodic interval*.

It is theoretically possible to have a large number of different pitches between a tone and its octave. However, the music of the Western world is based on a fairly equal division of the octave into twelve pitches, exclusive of the upper tone of the octave. This is shown schematically in Fig. 14. In Western music, the interval from any pitch to the next higher or lower pitch is called a *semitone*.

Fig. 14

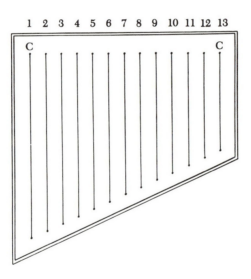

Any series of pitches arranged in order of successively higher or lower tones is called a *scale*. The zither-like instrument illustrated in Fig. 14, on which every successive string vibrates one-twelfth faster, produces a scale with twelve tones called the *chromatic scale*. Similar instruments with more or fewer strings, tuned in a variety of ways, have existed from ancient times. These instruments were played by plucking the strings, or by striking the strings with a pair of small hammers held in the hands. Ultimately a set of levers or *keys* were devised which extended under the strings and struck or plucked them with a projection fixed to the end of the key. Such keyboard instruments, encompassing at first a small and eventually a wider range of tones, evolved into the clavichord and harpsichord, predecessors of the modern piano.

Fig. 15 shows the arrangement of the piano keyboard. There are two kinds of keys, black and white. Starting from the key lettered C in Fig. 15, the black keys are grouped in a set of two and a set of three. Simple letter names from A to G are used for the white keys; the black keys have no independent letter names. A black key is identified with reference to the white key to the right and to the left of it. These two points of reference give each black key two pitch names, as is shown in Fig. 16.

Fig. 15

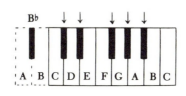

Fig. 16

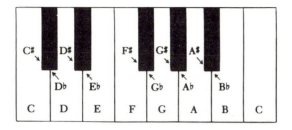

The black key to the right of C is higher in pitch than C and is called C-sharp, designated C♯. The term *sharp* means a semitone *higher* in pitch than the white key with the same letter name. This same black key is also a semitone below D in pitch. It is therefore called D-flat (D♭) as well, the term *flat* indicating it is a half-step *lower* in pitch than D. There is no black key between E and F or B and C to serve as E♯ and B♯. Since the second of each of these pairs of tones is a half-step higher than the first, F can be called E♯, and C, B♯. Under circumstances to be explained, you will find that such renaming of these keys is logical and necessary. Also, of course, going down the scale, E can be called F-flat, and B, C-flat. The circumstances which require that any black key be called sharp rather than flat, or vice versa, will be explained later.

Play the tones from C to C on the white keys, as shown in Fig. 16. This series of tones is the *C major scale*. It is unlike the chromatic scale in two respects: (1) the major scale has seven tones, the chromatic scale twelve (both exclusive of the octave tone); and (2) the C major scale has only two half steps, E-F and B-C; the rest of the tones are a *whole step* (two semitones) apart, while the chromatic scale is composed entirely of semitones. Fig. 17 separates the C major scale tones to make their relationship clearer.

Fig. 17

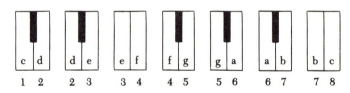

1 2   2 3   3 4   4 5   5 6   6 7   7 8

A major scale may start on any tone. It must conform to the pattern of whole and half steps given in Fig. 17, namely:

1st tone	2nd tone	3rd tone	4th tone	5th tone	6th tone	7th tone	8th tone
	whole step	*whole step*	*half step*	*whole step*	*whole step*	*whole step*	*half step*

The scale tones of any key are named as follows: 1, *tonic;* 2, *supertonic;* 3, *mediant;* 4, *subdominant;* 5, *dominant;* 6, *submediant;* 7, *leading tone.* Syllables are also used to refer to scale tones; these are: 1, *do;* 2, *re;* 3, *mi;* 4, *fa;* 5, *sol;* 6, *la;* 7, *ti;* 8, *do.*

Ex. 4a.   Play the C major scale on the piano. Start with the lowest C on the piano which you can comfortably sing. As you play each successive tone of the C major scale, sing the tone with *la,* making sure that your tone clearly matches the piano tone. Pause between tones to check yourself for exact intonation. Now sing up the scale, substituting scale-step numbers for the syllable *la.*

Ex. 4b.   Start from the octave tone and sing down the scale, first using *la,* then scale-step numbers 8, 7, 6, 5, etc. When you are certain that your pitches match the piano tones perfectly, play C, sing D, play D, sing E, play E, etc., checking your intonation after each tone with the piano.

Tonality

Play the beginning of *My Country, 'Tis of Thee* on these keys of the piano: C-C-D-B̄ (below C) C-D, E-E-F-E-D-C, D-C-B̄-C. Observe that the tone C is used more often than any other, and that the fragment of melody starts and ends with C. Play the same tones, stopping on the last B̄. The tendency of this tone to move on or *resolve* to C is unmistakable. These characteristics make the tone C the central and most stable tone of a whole group of tones, the C major scale. When a series of tones emphasize, center around, or mark one particular tone as a satisfying conclusion, we say a *tonality* is set up, meaning a central tone is felt to have other tones related to it as in a family. The C major scale is the tonality of C; a melody composed of the tones of that scale is in the tonality or *key* of C. (We have hitherto used the term *key* to mean one of the keyboard levers. Henceforth the term will mainly be used as applied in this paragraph.)

Elementary factors in learning to sing a melody from the printed page are: (1) knowing the letter names of the notes on the printed page; (2) identifying the scale step of each melody note; (3) being able to sing from any scale step to another up or down; (4) being able to sing the tones in the correct rhythm.

Students who are insufficiently acquainted with the notes on the printed page should study Fig. 19 and practice note-reading by reading the notes by letter name. Practice in reading melodies by scale-step numbers is given in succeeding exercises. Our first objective is to learn to sing from any scale step to another scale step.

Since the first scale step or *tonic tone* is the central tone of a key, we learn to sing other tones in the key by their *relationship to, and their feeling of distance from, that tone.* Being able to identify tones by ear and sing tones from the page in this manner is called using *relative pitch.*

Scale Tone Exercises

In the following exercises, a line over a number ($\overline{7}, \overline{5}$) means *that* scale step below the tonic; a line under a number ($\underline{2}, \underline{3}$) means *that* tone above the octave tonic. If the tones in this and succeeding exercises fall below your vocal range, start with a higher tonic tone.

Ex. 4c. Using the C major scale or any major scale given in this chapter which is convenient to your vocal range, strike the tonic tone and then practice singing the following scale steps: 1-2-3; 1-2-3-2-1; 1-2-1-3-1;

1-3-2-3-1; 1-3-2-1; 1-$\overset{\frown}{3}$ (hold the 3 and think 1); 1-2-3-4; 1-2-3-4-3; 1-2-1-3-1-4-1-3; 1-3-4-3; 1-2-4-3; 1-4-3; 1-4-3-2-1; 1-4-1-2; 1-4-2-3;

1-$\overset{\frown}{4}$ (hold the 4 and think 1). 1-2-3-4-5; 1-2-1-3-1-4-1-5; 1-2-3-5;

1-3-4-5; 1-3-5; 1-3-4-3-5; 1-3-2-5; 1-4-3-5; 1-2-4-3-5; 1-4-2-5; 1-$\overset{\frown}{5}$ (hold the 5 and think 1); 1-5-4-3-2-1; 1-5-4-3-1; 1-5-3-2-1; 1-5-4-2-3-1; 1-5-3-4-3; 1-5-2-3-1; 1-5-2-3-4; 1-5-2-4-3.

Ex. 4d. Follow the directions of Ex. 4c, with these scale steps: 1-$\bar{7}$-1; 1-$\bar{7}$-1-2-1; 1-$\bar{7}$-2-1; 1-2-$\bar{7}$-1; 1-$\bar{7}$-1-2-4-3; 1-$\bar{7}$-2-4-3; 1-$\bar{7}$-4-3; 1-3-4-3-1-$\bar{7}$-1; 1-4-3-1-$\bar{7}$-1; 1-4-$\bar{7}$-1; 1-4-3-2-$\bar{7}$-1; 1-4-2-$\bar{7}$-1; 1-5-1-$\bar{7}$-1; 1-5-$\bar{7}$-1; 1-5-4-$\bar{7}$-1; 1-5-4-3-2-$\bar{7}$-1; 1-5-4-2-$\bar{7}$-1; 1-5-2-4-$\bar{7}$-1; 1-5-2-$\bar{7}$-4-3; 1-$\bar{7}$-$\bar{6}$-$\bar{5}$-1; 1-$\bar{5}$-1; 1-$\bar{7}$-1-$\bar{5}$-1; 1-$\bar{7}$-$\bar{5}$-1; 1-$\bar{5}$-$\bar{7}$-1; 1-$\bar{7}$-1-$\bar{6}$-1-$\bar{5}$-1; 1-$\bar{5}$-$\bar{6}$-$\bar{5}$-1; 1-$\bar{5}$-$\bar{6}$-$\bar{7}$-$\bar{6}$-$\bar{5}$-1; 1-$\bar{5}$-$\bar{6}$-$\bar{7}$-$\bar{5}$-1; 1-$\bar{5}$-$\bar{7}$-$\bar{5}$-1; 1-$\overset{\frown}{\bar{5}}$ (hold the $\bar{5}$ and think 1).

Ex. 4e. Follow the directions of Ex. 4c with these scale steps: 1-2-1-$\bar{5}$-1; 1-2-$\bar{5}$-1; 1-2-3-1-$\bar{5}$-1; 1-2-3-$\bar{5}$-1; 1-3-$\bar{5}$-1; 1-$\bar{5}$-1-3; 1-$\bar{5}$-3-1; 1-3-4-3-$\bar{5}$-1; 1-4-3-$\bar{5}$-1; 1-4-$\bar{5}$-1; 1-4-3-2-$\bar{5}$-1; 1-4-2-$\bar{5}$-1; 1-4-2-1-$\bar{7}$-$\bar{5}$-1; 1-4-2-$\bar{7}$-$\bar{5}$-1; 1-$\bar{7}$-5; 1-$\bar{7}$-2-1-5; 1-$\bar{7}$-2-5; 1-$\bar{7}$-2-4-3-5; 1-$\bar{7}$-2-4-5-3; 1-$\bar{7}$-4-2-5-3; 1-5-3-4-2-3-1-2-$\bar{7}$-1; 1-5-1-$\bar{5}$-1; 1-5-$\bar{5}$-1; 1-5-1-$\bar{7}$-$\bar{5}$-1; 1-5-$\bar{7}$-$\bar{5}$-1; 1-5-2-$\bar{7}$-$\bar{5}$-1; 1-5-2-4-$\bar{7}$-$\bar{5}$-1; 1-5-4-2-$\bar{7}$-$\bar{5}$-1; 1-5-$\bar{7}$-2-$\bar{5}$-1; 1-5-$\bar{5}$-2-$\bar{7}$-1; 1-5-$\bar{5}$-$\bar{7}$-2-1; 1-5-$\bar{5}$-2-4-3; 1-4-2-$\bar{7}$-$\bar{5}$-5-1; 1-5-2-4-$\bar{7}$-2-$\bar{5}$-1.

Ex. 4f. Follow the directions of Ex. 4c with these scale steps: 1-2-3-4-5-$\overset{\frown}{6}$ (hold the 6)-5; 1-3-4-5-6-5; 1-3-5-6-5; 1-5-6-5; 1-2-3-4-6-5; 1-2-6-5; 1-3-6-5; 1-4-6-5; 1-2-4-6-5; 1-$\bar{7}$-1-6-5; 1-$\bar{7}$-6-5; 1-6-5-1; 1-6-5-3-1; 1-6-5-4-3-1; 1-6-4-3-1; 1-6-3-1; 1-6-1-2; 1-6-2-3; 1-6-1-$\bar{7}$-1; 1-6-$\bar{7}$-1; 1-6-4-2-$\bar{7}$-1; 1-6-5-$\bar{5}$-1; 1-6-$\bar{5}$-1.

Exercises 4c through 4f must be practiced until they can be sung with ease.

Notation

Music notation representing tones on the piano is written on two sets of five lines called the *great staff*, Fig. 18a. A center line between these sets, shown in Fig. 18a as a broken line, is used to locate the tone C near the middle of the keyboard, called *middle C*. Middle C is written on a small part of that line. The heavy lines in Fig. 18b designate two other fixed tones, G above middle C on the second line of the upper or *treble staff* and F below middle C on the fourth line of the lower or *bass staff*.

The symbol 𝄞, in Fig. 18c, placed on the treble staff with its tail

Fig. 18

end curling around the second line, is called the *treble clef*. The symbol 𝄢, which hangs from the fourth line of the bass staff in Fig. 18c is called the *bass clef*. Practice writing these clefs.

Music for the soprano and alto voice and for high-pitched instruments like the flute and violin, is written on the treble staff. Music for basses, baritones, and low-pitched instruments like the double bass, cello, and bassoon is written on the bass staff. Music for tenors is written on the bass staff when the great staff is used in four-part choral music. It is also written on the treble staff with a double G clef, 𝄞𝄞 , meaning "Read the notes in the G staff, but sing them an octave lower."

Students who are unsure of the notes on these staves should study them in three small groups, as shown in Fig. 19. The arrows show that middle C lies in the middle of the tonal range between the highest normal soprano note and the lowest normal bass note. Middle C is also approximately in the middle of the piano range.

Fig. 19

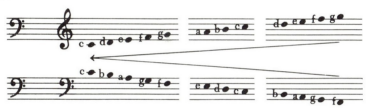

Play the tones on the white keys from G to G (see Fig. 20a). Observe that the tones sound like a major scale except for the next-to-last tone, which is a whole step from G. Substituting F♯ for F gives us the G major scale. The tone is designated F♯ rather than G♭, because in a major scale no letter may be omitted (E-G♭ omits F), nor any repeated (G♭ and G).

Fig. 20a

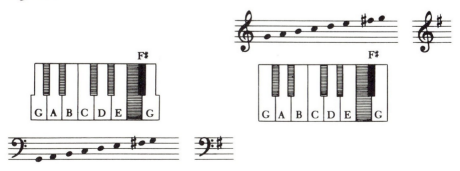

Fig. 20b

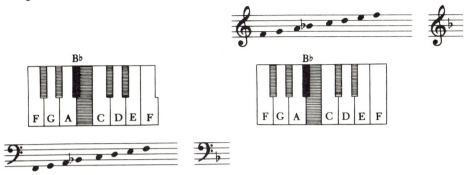

Fig. 20c

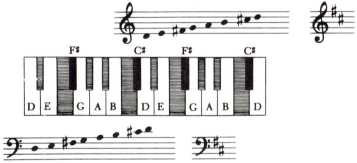

Fig. 20d

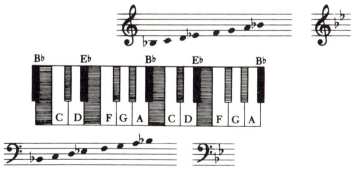

Play the tones on the white keys from F to F (see Fig. 20b). Here the tone B♭ (half step 3-4) must be substituted for B, to get the F major scale. The marked keys in Figs. 20a–d show the scale tones of the G major, F major, D major, and B♭ major scales.

Ex. 4g.   Write out Ex. 4c in the keys of G, F, D, and B♭, in treble and bass. *Do not copy the numbers used in the exercise under the notes*. Writing scale steps in notes is invaluable in learning to recognize any scale step in any key; it also accelerates the process of being able to take melodic dictation. Sing the notes you have written.

Key Signature

The F♯ required for the scale of G major is placed after the G clef on the fifth line and after the F clef on the fourth line. The composer writing a piece in the key of G thus avoids the necessity of writing a sharp sign before each F, because it is then understood that each F will be played or sung as F♯. Sharps or flats required for other scales are similarly placed after each clef, and are called *key signatures* (see Figs. 20a–d). Memorize the key signatures of G, F, D, and B♭ major.

Ex. 4h.   Write the major scales on the treble and bass staves of the following keys: A, E♭, E, A♭, B, D♭, F♯, G♭, G♯, C♯. Write out the key signatures for each key. The order in which sharps are added to key signatures is: F♯, C♯, G♯, D♯, A♯, E♯, B♯. The order in which flats are added to key signatures is: B♭, E♭, A♭, D♭, G♭, C♭.

Interval Practice

A melody can be sung with scale-step numbers (by relative pitch) when all of its tones are in a single key or when some are in a near-related key (p. 141). Frequent and unusual key changes occur in some melodies, making it difficult to identify the keys in the absence of the accompaniment. Singing such melodies by scale-step numbers is clearly impractical. In contemporary melody a sense of key often is absent. Both types of melody are best approached with a sure sense of interval—the ability to recognize and sing an interval of any size up or down with assurance.

Minor and Major Seconds

The major scale, as we have seen, is composed of whole and half steps, that is, tones and semitones. Fig. 21a illustrates half steps or semitones. When a semitone is composed of two tones with consecutive letters, such as B-C or C♯-D, the interval is called a *minor second*. (The terms *major* and *minor* when applied to intervals simply mean larger or smaller.) The minor second upward sounds like scale steps 7-8, *ti-do*. The minor second down sounds like scale steps 8-7, *do-ti*.

Ex. 5a.   Strike tones at random on the piano, calling each 7; then sing the minor second up as 8. Use Fig. 21a as a guide. Repeat this, singing both tones with *la*. Play the tones of the chromatic scale, calling each successive tone 7, then sing 8; C-D♭ (7-8), C♯-D (7-8), etc.

Ex. 5b.   Sing minor seconds down, again striking tones at random on the piano. Check your singing with Fig. 21a. Use *la* for both tones. Sing minor seconds down chromatically.

A *whole* step composed of two tones with consecutive letters, as C-D or E-F♯, is an interval of a *major second*. Fig. 21b illustrates whole steps. Scale steps 1-2, *do-re*, form a major second.

Ex. 5c.   Strike tones at random on the piano calling each 1; then sing 2. Use Fig. 21b to check your accuracy. Sing both tones with *la*. Sing up by consecutive major seconds: C-D, D-E, E-F♯, F♯-G♯, G♯-A♯, A♯-B♯ (C).

Ex. 5d.   Sing major seconds down from tones struck at random (2-1), then sing these tones with *la*. Practice singing a series of major seconds down, C-B♭, B♭-A♭, A♭-G♭, F♯-E, E-D, D-C.

Ex. 5e.   Name by letter a minor second up from the following notes: A, F♯, D, G, C♯, E, C, G♯, B, D♯, F, A♯, E♯, B♯; also B♭, E♭, G♭, A♭. In the last two, use a double flat, ♭♭, with the next letter name.

Ex. 5f.   Name by letter a minor second down from each letter in Ex. 5e.

Ex. 5g.   Name by letter a major second up from each letter in Ex. 5e.*

Ex. 5h.   Name by letter a major second down from each letter in Ex. 5e.

Ex. 5i.   Sing alternately major, then minor, seconds up; major and minor seconds down.

Fig. 21

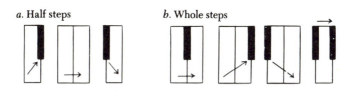

a. Half steps   *b*. Whole steps

Ledger Lines

In Ex. 4d we wrote the tones below middle C on the bass staff. Tones below middle C may be written in the treble staff by borrowing lines from the bass staff, as illustrated in Fig. 22a. Conversely, tones above middle C may be written in the bass staff by borrowing lines from the treble staff; see Fig. 22b. These borrowed, additional lines above or below either staff are called *ledger lines*.

* For E♯ and B♯, use a double sharp (✕).

Fig. 22

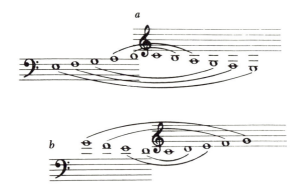

Ex. 6a.   Memorize the ledger lines in Fig. 22.

Ex. 6b.   Write out the notes in Ex. 4d in the keys of B♭ and D, using ledger lines below the treble staff.

Ex. 6c.   Write out the notes in Ex. 4f in the keys of A♭ and G, using ledger lines above the bass staff.

Scale Tone Exercises

In Ex. 4c, each series of tones started from the tonic tone. Melodies often begin on the third or fifth scale step. The following exercises develop facility in starting on these scale steps.

Ex. 7a.   Play C (scale step 1) on the piano; sing: 3-2-3-5, 3-2-3-6, 3-2-3-7, 3-2-3-8; 3-5-4-3, 6-5-3, 7-6-3, 8-5-3; 3-4-3-$\bar{5}$, 3-4-3-$\bar{6}$, 3-4-3-$\bar{7}$, 3-4-3-1. Play C on the piano; sing 5-6-5-4, 5-6-5-3, 5-6-5-2, 5-6-5-1, 5-6-5-$\bar{7}$, 5-6-5-$\bar{5}$-1, $\bar{5}$-$\bar{6}$-$\bar{5}$-$\bar{7}$, $\bar{5}$-$\bar{6}$-$\bar{5}$-1, $\bar{5}$-$\bar{6}$-$\bar{5}$-2, $\bar{5}$-$\bar{6}$-$\bar{5}$-3, $\bar{5}$-$\bar{6}$-$\bar{5}$-4, $\bar{5}$-$\bar{6}$-$\bar{5}$-5, 1.

Ex. 7b.   Write out the scale tones in Ex. 7a in the key of C; sing from the notes you have written.

Ex. 7c.   Repeat Ex. 7b in the following keys: G, E♭, A, D♭, B, F.

The Tonic Triad

A *chord* is composed of three or more tones sounded together. A three-tone chord is called a *triad*. Scale tones 1-3-5 form the *tonic triad*, or the *I chord*. The single tones of this triad are called: 1, root; 3, chord third; 5, chord fifth. The tones of the I chord—or any other chord—may be arranged so that any of the tones is the lowest note:

a. 5	b. 8 (1)	c. 3
3	5	1
1 (root)	3 (third)	5 (fifth)

The first arrangement, *a*, is the *fundamental order*. The second, *b*, is called the *first inversion;* the third, *c*, is called the *second inversion*. The symbol for *a* is I; the first inversion is indicated by I^6; the second inversion is indicated by I$^6_4$. The ^{6} in I^6 means that the root is six letter tones up from the bass note; the $^6_4$ in I$^6_4$ indicates that the root and third are respectively four and six letter tones up from the bass note.

Ex. 7d. Write the tonic triad in fundamental order, first inversion, and second inversion from each note given in Fig. 23.

Fig. 23

The tones of a chord sung in succession form a *broken chord*. Composers frequently use skips in the melody which are the separate tones of the I and other chords. Recognizing a series of tones in a melody as belonging to a single chord makes sight singing easier.

Ex. 7e. Sing the broken-chord tones of the I chord in C given in Fig. 24, first with scale-step numbers, then with *la*. Write out Fig. 24 in the bass staff, then sing with *la*.

Fig. 24

Ex. 7f. Write out each I chord of Ex. 7d in the patterns given in Fig. 24, then sing the tones with *la*.

The Dominant Triad

The scale tones 5-7-<u>2</u> in combination form a triad on the fifth scale step which is called the *dominant triad* or *V chord*. This triad normally resolves—that is, moves on—to the I chord. Some melodies begin with tones of the V triad.

Ex. 7g. Considering each note of Fig. 23 as a tonic tone, write out the V triad in each key, in fundamental order, in first, and in second, inversions.

Ex. 7h. Write the V chords of Ex. 7g, following the patterns given in Fig. 24.

Ex. 7i. The following scale steps combine tones of the I and V. Write them out in C and in several other major keys; sing the tones from your notes: 1-3-5, 5̄-7̄-2, 1; 1-5-3, 2-7̄-5̄, 1; 3-5-1, 5̄-2-7̄, 1; 1, 7̄-2-5̄, 5-3-1; 1, 5-7̄-2, 3-5-8; 1, 2-7̄-2-5, 5-1-3.

The Major Third; The Perfect Fifth

The interval from root to third of the I and V is a *major third*. The tones of every major third are two whole steps apart. Major scale steps 1-3, 3-1, 4-6, 6-4, 5-7, and 7-5 are skips of a major third. On the music staff a skip of a third is from a line to the next line above or below; or from a space to the next space above or below. Major thirds must be two whole steps apart and encompass three letters; for example, C-D-E.

Ex. 8a. Name by letter (including any necessary sharps or flats) a major third up from each note in Fig. 23. Sing a major third up from each tone, checking your accuracy.

Ex. 8b. Name by letter a major third down from each note in Fig. 23. Sing these scale steps, 3-2-1, 3-1. Sing a major third down from each note in Fig. 23.

The interval from root to fifth of the I and V chords is a *perfect fifth*. The tones of the perfect fifth are three-and-a-half steps apart, and encompass five letters. With the exception of scale steps 7̄-4 and 4-7̄, five letters up or down from any major scale tone is a perfect fifth. On the staff, when a note is on a line, a perfect fifth lies two lines above or below; the perfect fifth lies two spaces above or below a note in a space. Major triads are composed of a lower major third and a perfect fifth.

Ex. 8c.　Name by letter a perfect fifth up from each note in Fig. 23. Sing these scale tones: 1-5̄; 1-5̄-2; 3-4-8; 1-5, 2-6, 3-7-8. Sing a perfect fifth up from each tone in Fig. 23 with *la*.

Ex. 8d.　Name by letter a perfect fifth down from each note in Fig. 23. Sing these scale tones: 5-1; 2-5̄-1; 8-4, 7-3, 6-2, 3-6̄; conclude with 5̄-1. Sing a perfect fifth down from each note in Fig. 23.

One important objective of ear training is to develop the ability to identify chords by ear. A first step toward achieving this is to learn how to identify intervals by ear. This entails hearing both tones of an interval and then judging the size of the interval. Exercise 9 affords practice in hearing the bottom tones of intervals.

Ex. 9.　Play each interval in Fig. 25 on the piano, with equal stress on both tones; sing the *bottom* tone of each interval. If you find this difficult, raise the top tone or lower the bottom tone by an octave, then try the original tones again.

Fig. 25

Nonharmonic Tones; The Passing Tone

Play the familiar fragment of melody and its accompaniment given in Fig. 26a.

Fig. 26a.

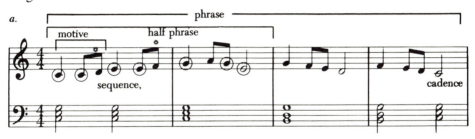

Fig. 26b.

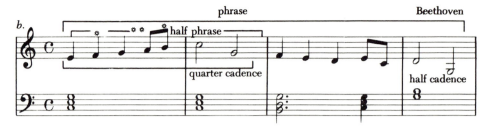

The circled tones in Fig. 26a are *chord tones*, that is, they duplicate the chord tones of the accompaniment. The other tones are *nonchord* or *nonharmonic* tones. None of the tones in Fig. 26a or Fig. 26b would be nonharmonic if each of them was harmonized with a different chord. The identification of nonharmonic tones in unaccompanied melody is therefore subject to uncertainty. Nonharmonic tones are classified according to the way they function in relation to chord tones.

The starred tones in Fig. 26a and 26b are used to pass scalewise from one chord tone to another; tones with this function are called *diatonic passing tones*. *Diatonic* indicates that these tones occur in the scale represented by the key signature, as opposed to *chromatic tones* which do not belong to the scale of the signature. Passing tones which fall on an unaccented beat, or on the last half or last fraction of a beat, are called *unaccented passing tones*. The double-starred tone in Fig. 26b is an *accented passing tone*. A series of scale tones may thus function as passing tones filling the gaps between chord tones.

Ex. 10a.   Find the tones which appear to be passing tones in the melodies in Section 1, p. 47. They are usually tones of short duration.

Auxiliary Tones

A group of three tones may consist of a chord tone, a tone which moves up or down by step from the chord tone, and a return to the original chord tone. The middle tone in such a group is called an *auxiliary* or *neighboring tone*. When the tone moves up from the original chord tone, it is called an *upper auxiliary*, abbreviated UA; when the tone moves down, it is called a *lower auxiliary*, abbreviated LA. Upper and lower auxiliaries are illustrated in Fig. 27.

Fig. 27

The symbol ⤳ over a note indicates a rapid auxiliary figure with an upper auxiliary; the symbol ⤳ indicates a similar figure with the lower auxiliary.

Ex. 10b. Sing the following auxiliary tones of the I, starting on any convenient tonic note: 1-2-1; 3-4-3; 5-6-5; 1-7̄-1; 3-2-3; 5-4-5, 3.

Ex. 10c. Sing the tones of the V with passing tones: 1, 5̄-6̄-7̄, 1; 5, 7̄-1-2, 1; 3, 2-1-7̄, 1; 5, 7̄-6̄-5̄, 1; and with auxiliaries: 1, 5̄-6̄-5̄, 1; 5, 7̄-1-7̄-5̄; 5̄, 2-3-2, 1; 5-6-5, 2-3-2, 7̄-1-7̄, 1; 8, 7-6-7, 5-4-5, 2-1-2, 3.

Melodic and Rhythmic Dictation

The difficulty which students may experience in writing down melody and rhythm from dictation is at least partially attributable to their faulty procedure. The following suggestions will be helpful:

1. *Do not start writing the tones immediately;* you may set down a few tones and forget the rest. You cannot write correctly what you cannot remember or what has been faultily memorized. Memorize the dictated portion of melody by singing it quietly or in your mind, two or three times.

Some students find memorization difficult. This can be improved with persistent and regular practice. Play two-measure units from the melodies for sight singing. Look away from the book and sing them, then check for accuracy. When you can do this well, take four-measure units. Better still, work with another student, taking turns in dictating.

2. Determine whether the melody begins on 1, 3, or 5 by singing 1; then check the first tone of the melody against these three tones. Beginning with the wrong tone will make the following tones wrong.

3. Set down the correct key signature, then write the scale-step numbers for the dictated melody. If you are proficient enough, write the tones (without the rhythm) directly. Note the parts which move

scalewise up or down. Note the skips which run along tonic-chord lines. Skips to tones other than 1, 3, or 5 lie one tone above or below one of these three tones; for example, 4-3, 6-5, $\overline{7}$-1 or 7-8, 2-1, or 2-3. Sing 1; is the tone above or below? Sing 3; is the tone above or below? Sing 5, etc. *Always check against these three tones.*

4. Set down the meter, listening for the strong beat; count the number of unaccented beats. Place a bar line before every tone on an accented beat. This will give you the correct number of tones within each measure. Note whether the first tone comes on beat 1, or whether it is an up beat note.

5. Now determine the rhythm in each measure. As a temporary expedient you may use dashes to represent the duration of the tones as in Fig. 28:

Fig. 28

First write the rhythm for tones with simple durations of one beat or two beats; then for those which run over a beat or which divide a beat.

Consistent use of this approach will make taking dictation quick and automatic.

Elementary Form

Musically intelligent sight reading requires more than note-to-note reading. It is essential to be able to recognize rapidly various structural factors such as the repetition of melodic units, cadences, chord skips, and so on. The student will learn to perceive these and other factors with practice in analysis. He must also cultivate the habit of looking ahead.

Tones and time, when organized in patterns, are the materials for creating music. Scales are organized tone patterns. Melodies consisting merely of scale tones moving up or down in order are uninteresting and consequently rare. Some melodies, like *Joy to the World* and *The First Nowell*, may start out by moving scalewise; later, however, the order of the tones is varied. Or the first tones of a melody may consist of a scale fragment, as in Fig. 26a. Many melodies start with skips in the tonic chord.

The Motive and Motive Repetition

The pattern of the first three tones in Fig. 26a is repeated in the next three tones. A group of tones which serve as the generating core of a melody is called a *motive*. Motives, the smallest coherent units of melody, are usually from two to about seven or eight tones in length.

The composer who starts with a motive may evolve the melody in one of several ways. He may (1) repeat it exactly; (2) repeat it and change the rhythm, or a note or two, which is called a *modified repetition;* (3) shift the motive to a higher or lower level (as in Fig. 26a), a pattern called a *sequence;* (4) employ the sequence with rhythmic or tonal changes, called a *modified sequence.*

Another way to evolve melody is to follow the first motive (with or without repetitions) with one or more different motives. Repetitions of one kind or another provide unity; some offer variety. New motives provide contrast.

Ex. 11a.   Look through the melodies in Section 2, p. 60, to find examples of the types of motive repetition and expansion described in the text.

Ex. 11b.   Analyze the first two measures of melodies in Section 2, looking for contrasting motives.

Ex. 11c.   Study the melodies in Section 2 to find examples of skips in I and V.

The Cadence; The Phrase; The Period

The melodic line, continued beyond the initial motive by repetitions or additional motives, may break, then continue on its way. This break, usually on a tone held for more than one beat, is called a *cadence;* see Figs. 26a and 26b. Cadences may appear after two or more measures of music. Ordinarily cadences fall in the second, fourth, and/or eighth measures, but this is a matter which is governed partly by tempo and meter. The melodic unit from the first tone up to and including the cadence tone is called a *phrase;* see Fig. 26b. Some phrases have a slight break at or near the middle; this break is a *quarter cadence,* and the two parts of the phrase are *half phrases* (Figs. 26a and b).

Phrases may be irregular in length—that is, three, five, six, or seven measures long. Irregular phrases occur in contemporary melody and in some types of folk music.

Cadences which end on a tone of the V chord are called *half cadences,* or *semicadences.* Those which end on a tone of the I are *authentic cadences.* In accompanied melody, cadences on 5 or 3, with the underlying I chord preceded by V, are called *imperfect authentic cadences.* The *perfect authentic cadence* has the tonic tone in the melody and the I in fundamental order in the bass.

Ex. 11d.   Identify the cadences in the melodies in Section 2.

Phrase Formations

A two-phrase unit is called a *period*. Just as a motive may be repeated exactly or with some modification, so may the phrase be repeated. The only difference in the repetition may be in the cadences; or the second phrase may be exactly like the first, or a modified version, or a sequence of it. Looking ahead of the measure you are singing will apprise you of what to expect.

Ex. 11e.   Examine the melodies in Section 2 for types of phrase repetition.

A new motive may follow a first motive, and similarly, a new phrase may follow the first phrase. Some folk tunes are constructed in this simple pattern: phrase 1 (A), phrase 2 (B). This pattern is *simple binary form:* A, B. One or both phrases may be repeated: A-A-B; A-B-B; A-A-B-B; A-B-A-B.

More common than binary is *simple ternary form*, A-B-A, which is evenly balanced when the first A is repeated: A-A-B-A. Variants of simple ternary form are: A-B-B-A; A-A-B-B-A. Any repeated phrase in these forms may be modified. A second or a third new phrase may follow A or B, such as A-A-B-C, A-B-B-C, A-B-C-C, A-B-A-C, A-B-C-B, A-B-C-D.

Ex. 11f.   Analyze the structure of the melodies in Section 2.

Phrase, Period, and Sectional Repetition Signs

When a phrase, a period, or an entire section is repeated, either exactly, with changes in the beginning, or with changes in the cadences, the composer spares himself the trouble of writing out the repeated parts by employing various repetition signs. A double bar with two dots at the end of a phrase or period means, "Go back to the beginning":

Fig. 29

If a repetition is desired without the first one or two measures, or more commonly, without the upbeat note or notes, the place to which the return is made is marked by the same sign facing the other way:

Fig. 30

When the melody starts with one or more upbeat notes, the phrase or period after the repetition generally also begins with upbeat notes. In this case, the first cadence note is less than a measure long, the repeat sign falls within the cadence measure, and the rest of that measure has upbeat notes for the next phrase or section:

Fig. 31

In some pieces the middle or last phrase, period, or section is repeated: A-A-B-B, A-B-B-A, A-B-B-C, A-B-C-C; the repeat signs are placed accordingly:

Fig. 32

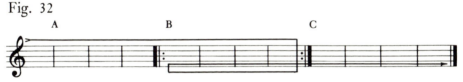

A repeated section of music may have two different endings, perhaps a semicadence for the first ending, and a perfect cadence for the second ending. Or, a first ending may be made in the original key and a second ending in a new key, or vice versa. For endings differing in this way, the first is marked ⌐1   :‖⌐ ; a return is made to the beginning; the performer sings up to ⌐1   :‖, skips *that* ending and takes ending ⌐2   . In some melodies the music continues from the second ending, as illustrated.

Fig. 33

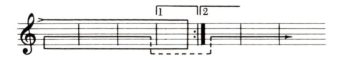

When a return is made to the beginning phrase or phrases after a different middle part, as in A-B-A or A-B-C-A-A-B, the composer can avoid writing out the repetitions by using the words, *Da Capo* (abbreviated *D.C.*) *al fine*, meaning "From the head (beginning) to the end."

Fig. 34

In some instances the repetition of the *last part only* of a given phrase, period, or section is required. The instruction, *Dal Segno* (abbreviated *D.S.*) *al fine* means "Return to the sign 𝄋 and sing to the close." When repeating a stanza of a song, the return to this sign eliminates a repetition of the piano introduction.

Fig. 35

The same sign is used when the *first* part of a phrase or period is repeated, the *last* part omitted, and the music skips to the next phrase. The instruction given is *Al Segno* (𝄋) *dal fine:* "From the sign to the close."

Fig. 36

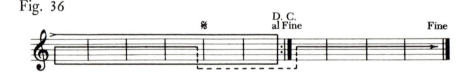

The sign ⊕ is more commonly used: (1) when neither cadence ⌐1   :‖⌐ nor ⌐2   provides a perfect cadence in the original key, thus requiring a third and final ending; (2) when an additional phrase, called a *codetta*, closes the piece; (3) when the sign 𝄋 has been used for an earlier repeat. The instruction given is *al Segno* (⊕) *dal Segno* (⊕).

Fig. 37

CHAPTER
3

Two-beat Syncopation

ANY tone which is longer in duration than the ones before and after it becomes rhythmically prominent. Such tones have a *durational accent*. Examine the rhythms in Ex. 3a. Observe that the two-beat values in simple triple meter start on the first beat; in simple quadruple meter they start either on the *primary accent*, beat 1, or on the *secondary accent*, beat 3. The mind readily accepts long tones starting on the metric or secondary accent because these durational accents either reinforce the metric accent or fall on the normal division of the measure.

When a long tone starts on an unaccented beat it sets up a durational accent which is in conflict with the normal metric accent:

Beats: 1   2   3   4   1

Tones: [music notation]

Or [music notation]

Rhythms with displaced two-beat values are another form of syncopation.* The following are examples of two-beat syncopations:

Short-long-short: 4/4 ♩ ♩ ♩   4/8 ♪ ♩ ♪   4/16 [notation]

Short-long-rest: ♩ ♩ ♩   ♪ ♩ ♪   [notation]

Rest-long-short: ♩ ♩ ♩   ♪ ♩ ♪   [notation]

Rest-long-rest: ♩ ♩ ♩   ♪ ♩ ♪   [notation]

Short-long: 3/4 ♩ ♩   3/8 ♪ ♩   3/8 ♪ ♪

Rest-long: 2/4 ♩ ♩ ♩   3/4 ♩ ♩   3/8 ♪ ♩

Rests which start on an unaccented beat and are similarly prolonged compel us to accent the silent beat inwardly as well as the offbeat tone following the rest:

4/4 ♩ ♩ ♩ | ♩ ♩
4/4 ♩ ♩ ♩ ♩ | ♩ ♩

Ex. 12a. Erase the penciled ties in Fig. 8; write in syncopated ties;

* For the present the tie will be used for two-beat notes in which the second beat is over the bar line, since a note or rest cannot straddle the bar line. Rests may be used within beamed notes: 4/8 [notation]; [notation], or [notation].

tie beats *across* the bar lines. As before, clap the rhythms, then sing with *la*.

Ex. 12b.   The rhythms in Fig. 38 are a little more difficult. Take a slow tempo, but keep the beats going steadily as you clap and sing the rhythms. Note that the rhythms: ♫♩ ; ♪♩♪ ; ♩♩♩ ; and ♩°♩ are proportionately the same in different meters. (The sign C which appears in the first line of Ex. 12b is often used to indicate 4/4 meter.)

Fig. 38

Ex. 12c. Clap four measures of each unit in Ex. 12b in turn, writing what you have clapped from memory.

Ex. 12d. Read each line of Ex. 12b silently.

Two-beat Values in Composite Meters

Ex. 12e. Clap the rhythms of Fig. 39 with a strong first-beat accent. Keep the beats steady; sing with *la*.

Fig. 39

Mixed Meters

Some contemporary composers put bar lines where dynamic accents occur; the result is a meter scheme which is called *mixed meter:*

```
          >           >      >              >  >
          1  2  3  |  1  2  3  |  1  2  3  |  1  2  3
becomes
          1  2  3  |  1  2  |  1  2  3  4  |  1  |1  2
  or
          3/4     |  2/4  |      4/4      |1/4| 2/4
```

A metric signature of 3/4 4/4 means that the music has measures of three and four beats, which do *not* alternate as in 7/4. When more than two different meters are used in a melody, the metric changes are indicated as in Fig. 40. Since people tend to feel comfortable in metric regularity, any deviations like those in Fig. 40, whether we find them disconcerting or stimulating, seize our attention.

Ex. 12f. Clap the rhythms of Fig. 40 in mixed meters without changing the pace of the beats, then sing with *la*.

Fig. 40

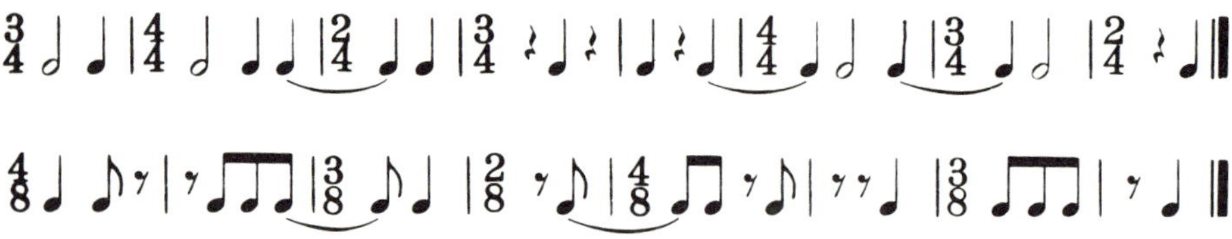

The Subdominant or IV Triad

The scale tones 4-6-8 in combination form the *IV chord* or *sub-dominant triad*. The I, V, and IV chords are the basic triads in the key. Among them they use all the tones of the scale. All are major-sounding chords.

Ex. 13a.   Considering each note in Fig. 23 a tonic note, write out the IV chord in fundamental order, first inversion, and second inversion, in all major keys.

Ex. 13b.   The following combinations include tones of the I-IV, IV-I, and IV-V chords. Write them out in C and several other major keys, then sing from your notes: 1-3-5, 1-4-6, 5; 5-3-1, 6-4-1, 3; 3-5-8, 8-6-4, 3; 3-5-8, 4-6-8, 5; $\overline{5}$-1-3, $\overline{6}$-1-4, 3; 1-6-4, 3-5-8; 1-4-6-8-5-3-1; 8-6-4, 3-5-1; 1-4-$\overline{6}$, $\overline{5}$-1-3; 1-$\overline{6}$-4, 3-5-8; $\overline{6}$-1-4-3-5-1; (IV-V) 3, 4-6-8, 7-5-$\underline{2}$-8; 1-6-4, 2-$\overline{7}$-5, 1; 1-4-6, 5-$\overline{7}$-2-1.

Ex. 13c.   The following tones combine IV chord tones with auxiliaries. Follow the directions in Ex. 13b: 1-$\overline{7}$-1, 4-3-4, 6-5-6, 5; 1-2-1, 4-5-4, 6-7-6, 5; 1-$\overline{7}$-1, 4-3-4, 6-7-6, 5.

Ex. 13d.   The following tones combine IV chord tones with passing tones. Follow the directions of Ex. 13b: 1-4-5-6, 5; 1-$\overline{6}$-$\overline{7}$-1, $\overline{5}$; 1-2-3-4-6, 5; 8-7-6-8-6, 5; 1, 6-5-4-6-4, 3.

The Perfect Fourth

Scale tones 1-4 form an interval of a *perfect fourth*. The perfect fourth is a half step larger than the major third and encompasses four letters, C-D-E-F. Four scale steps up from any tone except 4, and four scale steps down from any tone except 7, will be a skip of a perfect fourth. When a note is on a line, a fourth will be two spaces above or below it; when a note is in a space a fourth will be two lines above or below.

Ex. 14a.   Name by letter a perfect fourth up from each note in Fig. 23; then sing perfect fourths up from each tone with *la*. At the start you may find it necessary to think 1-4 or $\bar{5}$-1. Sing 1-4-2-5-3-6-5-8; $\bar{5}$-1-$\bar{6}$-2-$\bar{7}$-3, 5-8.

Ex. 14b. Name by letter a perfect fourth down from each note in Fig. 23, then sing perfect fourths down from each tone with *la*. At the start you may find it necessary to think 1-$\bar{5}$. This is easier than 4-1. Sing 8-5-6-3-4-1-2-$\bar{6}$-1-$\bar{5}$.

The Three-beat Value

The three-beat value in 3/2 and 4/2 is: ○ | 𝅗𝅥 (two beats plus one)

in 3/4 and 4/4   : 𝅗𝅥 | 𝅘𝅥

in 3/8 and 4/8   : 𝅘𝅥 | 𝅘𝅥𝅮

in 3/16 and 4/16: 𝅘𝅥𝅮 | 𝅘𝅥𝅯

Ties are mainly used when two of the beats lie on either side of the bar line. In 2/2 and 2/4 a whole-measure note is tied across the bar line. The three-beat note *within* the measure, however, is written as a dotted note: for example, $^3_4$/𝅘𝅥.. The nature of the symbol may be understood as a simplification of a tied three-beat note: 3/4 𝅘𝅥 𝅗𝅥 = 𝅗𝅥. = 𝅗𝅥. = 𝅗𝅥. The dot is applied also to rests: ▬· = ▬ + 𝄽 ; 𝄽· = 𝄽 + 𝄾 ; 𝄾· = 𝄾 + 𝄾 . The dot thus prolongs the duration of the note value by one-half its value. In simple triple meter such notes fill the measure; in quadruple meter they fill three-fourths of the measure.

Ex. 15a. Clap the rhythms in Fig. 41, holding the palms together for three beats on three-beat notes; then sing with *la*:

Fig. 41

Ex. 15b. Clap four measures of the first line of Fig. 41, then write it from memory. Do this with the second line, and with each line in the Figure.

Ex. 15c. Read Fig. 41 silently. The rhythms can be felt physically in your throat or in the abdominal muscles. Silent rhythm reading is a factor in learning to read a page of music and hear it mentally.

Note that rhythms like 4/8 ♪. ♪, 4/4 ♩. ♩, 4/2 𝅗𝅥. 𝅗𝅥 and 4/16 ♫ ♫ are proportionately the same in different meters.

Three-beat Values with Upbeat

Ex. 15d. Clap the rhythms in Fig. 42, then sing with *la*.

Ex. 15e. Write four-measure units of the lines in 3/8, 4/4, and 4/16 in Fig. 42 from memory.

Ex. 15f. Read the rhythms of Fig. 42 silently.

Fig. 42

* The sign ₵ is often used to indicate 2/2 meter.

CHAPTER THREE

Three-beat Values in Syncopation

Ex. 15g.   Clap the rhythms in Fig. 43, then sing with *la*. Write four-measure units from memory; read these rhythms silently.

Fig. 43

The Three-beat Value in Composite Meters

Ex. 15h.   Clap the rhythms in Fig. 44, keeping a steady beat, then sing with *la*. Read the rhythms silently; write the lines from memory.

Fig. 44

The Three-beat Value in Mixed Meters

Ex. 15i. Clap the rhythms in Fig. 45, keeping a steady beat; then sing
with *la:*

Fig. 45

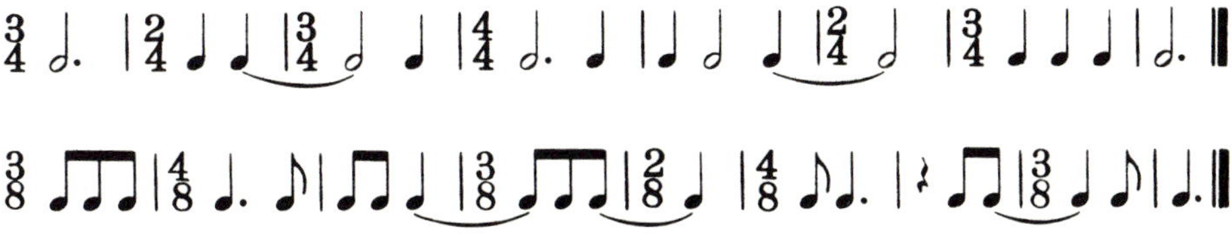

The Major Sixth

Sing the scale tones, 5̄-1, 1-3, 5̄-3. The skip 5̄-3 is an interval of a
major sixth. In major it appears in the I, 5̄-3; in the IV, 1-6; in the V, 2-7;
and in the II, 4-2̲ (see below, p. 93). The distance between tones is
equal to a perfect fourth plus a major third, or a perfect fifth plus a
whole step. The major sixth encompasses six letters, C-D-E-F-G-A.
When the first note of a skip is on a line, a sixth will be three spaces
above or below it; when it is in a space, a sixth will be three lines above
or below.

Ex. 16a. Name by letter a major sixth up from each note in Fig. 23.
Sing 5̄-1, 1-3, 5̄-3; sing 5̄-3, 1-6, 2-7, 8. Sing a major sixth up from
each tone in Fig. 23.

Ex. 16b. Name by letter a major sixth down from each note in Fig. 23.
Sing 3-1, 1-5̄, 3-5̄; 8-7-2, 6-1, 3-5̄, 1; 8,2̲-4, 3-5̄,1. Sing a major sixth
down from each tone in Fig. 23.

Ex. 16c. Review Exercises 5, 8, and 14.

Ex. 16d. Write out Ex. 4c in the keys of E♭ major and A major.

The Four-beat Value

In simple quadruple meter, the four-beat value either fills the measure
or is tied over the bar line. In simple duple and triple meter, it must be
tied over the bar line.

Ex. 17a. Clap the rhythms in Fig. 46, then sing with *la.* Note the
whole-measure rests (see Fig. 8) used in 3/4; the whole rest is used
for whole-measure rests in all meters.

Fig. 46

Ex. 17b. Clap the rhythms of Ex. 17a, then write each line from memory.

Ex. 17c. In Exercises 3a, 3b, 12b, 12e, 15a, 15d, 15g, 15h, and 17a, rhythms are presented in pairs of lines within each particular meter. Tap the rhythms of both lines simultaneously on the desk or table, the upper line with the right palm, the lower line with the left palm. Do all these exercises.

The Dominant Seventh Chord, V^7

The scale tones 5-7-2-4 or $\overline{5}$-$\overline{7}$-2-4, in combination, form the V^7 or *dominant seventh chord.* This chord, which is a V triad with a super-imposed third, has an interval of a minor seventh from its root, $\overline{5}$, to its chord seventh, 4. The chord normally resolves to I.

Fig. 47

$$V^6_5 \qquad V^4_3 \qquad V^2$$

The first inversion of V^7 written V^6_5 has the chord third in the bass; it normally resolves to I. The second inversion, written V^4_3 has the fifth in bass; it normally resolves to I or I^6. The third inversion, written V^2, has the seventh in bass; it resolves to I^6.

Ex. 18a. Considering each note in Fig. 23 as a tonic tone, write out the V^7 chord and its inversions in each key. Sing a dominant seventh chord up from each tone in Fig. 23.

Ex. 18b. Write out the following scale tones, centered on the V^7, in C: 1, $\overline{5}$-$\overline{7}$-2-4, 3; $\overline{5}$-4-$\overline{7}$-4-2-4, 3; 1, $\overline{7}$-2-4-5, 3; 1, 2-4-5-7, 8; 1, 4-2-$\overline{7}$-$\overline{5}$, 1; 1, 5-4-2-$\overline{7}$, 1; 8, 7-5-4-2, 3; 1, 4-2-5-$\overline{7}$, 1; 1-4-$\overline{7}$-2-5, 1; 1, 5-2-4-$\overline{7}$, 1; 1, $\overline{7}$-4-2-$\overline{5}$, 1; 1, $\overline{5}$-2-$\overline{7}$-4, 3; 1, $\overline{5}$-4-$\overline{7}$-2, 1.

Ex. 18c. The V^7 is used with auxiliaries in the following combinations; write them out in C: $\overline{5}$-$\overline{6}$-$\overline{5}$, $\overline{7}$-1-$\overline{7}$, 2-3-2, 4-5-4, 3; 5, 4-3-4, 2-1-2, $\overline{7}$-$\overline{6}$-$\overline{7}$, 1; $\overline{5}$-$\overline{6}$-$\overline{5}$, 2-3-2, $\overline{7}$-1-$\overline{7}$, 4-5-4, 3; 4-3-4, $\overline{7}$-$\overline{6}$-$\overline{7}$, 2-1-2-5, 1.

Ex. 18d. The V^7 is used with passing tones in the following combinations; write them out in C: 1, $\overline{5}$-$\overline{6}$-$\overline{7}$, $\overline{7}$-1-2, 2-3-4, 3; 1, $\overline{7}$-$\overline{6}$-$\overline{5}$, 2-1-$\overline{7}$, 4-3-2, 1; 8, 7-6-5, 2-3-4, $\overline{7}$-$\overline{6}$-$\overline{5}$, 1.

Ex. 18e. Sing the tones you have written. Write out all of Ex. 18 in the keys of F, G, D, and B♭.

The Minor Seventh

The skip $\overline{5}$-4 is an interval of a *minor seventh*. This is a half step larger than a major sixth. The minor seventh encompasses seven letters, G-A-B-C-D-E-F and is found in major keys between $\overline{5}$-4, $\overline{7}$-6, $\overline{6}$-5, 2-8, and 3-$\underline{2}$. When a note is on a line, a seventh will be three lines above or below it; when a note is in a space, a seventh will be three spaces above or below.

Ex. 18d.   Name by letter a minor seventh up from each note in Fig. 23, then sing minor sevenths up from each tone. Start by practicing $\overline{5}$-$\overline{7}$-2-4, $\overline{5}$-4.

Ex. 18e.   Name by letter a minor seventh down from each note in Fig. 23, then sing minor sevenths down from each tone. Start by practicing 4-2-$\overline{7}$-$\overline{5}$, 4-$\overline{5}$.

Ledger Lines, Continued

Tones higher than the G above the treble staff are notated on or between ledger lines above that staff, tones lower than the F below the bass staff are written on or between ledger lines below that staff. Learn the location of these notes, which are shown in Fig. 48a. These tones lie outside the normal vocal range. It is necessary to know them for instrumental playing, as well as for hearing instrumental music mentally.

Fig. 48a

The symbol $8_{\text{va}}\overline{}|$ is sometimes used over notes which are to be sounded an octave *higher* than written on the treble staff. The symbol $8_{\text{va}}\_\_\_\_|$ is used below notes in the bass which are to be sounded an octave *lower* than written. See Fig. 48b.

Fig. 48b

Ex. 18f.   Read the notes of the melodies of Section 1 by scale step numbers without singing them. Try to develop facility in reading them quickly, then sing the melodies.   Develop the habit of noticing key and metric signatures.

SECTION 1

Simple Melodies Employing Rhythmic Values in Chapters 1 and 3

48   SECTION 1

11 LENTO   NETHERLANDS

12 VIVACE   DITTERSDORF

13 MODERATO   CAVALLI

14 ALLEGRETTO ESTHONIA

15 ALLEGRO CON MOTO   BEETHOVEN

16 MODERE   FRANCE

17 SPIRITED   UNITED STATES

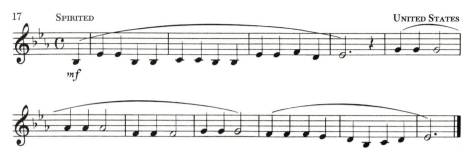

18   BOIELDIEU

19 THREE-VOICE CANON   SCHNEIDER

20 LIVELY   UNITED STATES

21 MODERATO   WENNERBERG

26   LARGO   SALIERI

27   ALLEGRO   SULLIVAN

28   SEHNSUCHTVOLL   CZECHOSLOVAKIA

29   ANDANTE   PURCELL

30   MODERATELY FAST   UNITED STATES

37 VIGOROUSLY   BARTOK

mf

38 ENERGETICALLY   WALTON

mf

39   LA PARRA

40 ANDANTE TRANQUILLO   DE FALLA

pp   p espr.

CHAPTER

4

Durations of a Fraction of a Beat

Two or more tones may occupy a single beat. When two tones, equal in value, take the place of a single-beat value, the second half beat is usually counted "and," in order to avoid stretching out the numbered counting into "wuh-one, tuh-oo, thre-ee, foh-our." In beating out these values, an extra loop is inserted in each stroke, thus dividing the beat.

The following schemes show half-beat values for the most common meters. In 2/16, 3/16, and 4/16, *thirty-second* notes are used; these look like sixteenth notes except that they have three beams. Detached thirty-second notes have three flags, and thirty-second rests have three hooks.

a.   Half-beat values for $\dfrac{2, 3, 4}{2}$

b.   Half-beat values for $\dfrac{2, 3, 4}{4}$

c.   Half-beat values for $\dfrac{2, 3, 4}{8}$

d.   Half-beat values for $\dfrac{2, 3, 4}{16}$

With half-beat rests:

Ex. 19a.   Clap the rhythms in Fig. 49, then sing with *la*. To insure

55

giving full value to whole-beat and two-beat values, count *all* the half-beats.

Fig. 49

Ex. 19b.   Using the first four lines of Ex. 19a, write four-measure units from memory.

Ex. 19c.   Study four-measure units of the last four lines of Ex. 19a. Write them from visual memory.

Durations of a Beat-and-a-Half

Notes with the duration value of a beat-and-a-half are written in two ways.

(1) The half-beat value may be tied to the whole beat:

3/4

1-and 2-and 3-and

(2) The note may be dotted: 3/4 ♩   . ♪   ♩

1-and 2-and 3-and, which is written as

3/4 ♩.   ♪   ♩
3/2 ♩.   ♩   ♩
3/8 ♩.   ♪   ♩

A beat-unit rest dotted is a beat-and-a-half long: 3/4 ♩. ♪ ♩ or ♩ ♪ ♩

Ex. 19d.   Clap the rhythms in Fig. 50, then sing with *la*. Note that the rhythms, ♩. ♩ , ♩. ♪ , ♫♪ ; and ♫♪ are proportionately the same in different meters.

Fig. 50

Ex. 19e.   Read four-measure units from each line of Fig. 50 silently, then write them from memory.

Half-beat Values in Syncopation

A syncopated rhythm involving half-beat values is formed when (1) the note on the *second* half of a beat is tied to one on the *first* half of the following beat: 2/4 ♫♪; (2) written as 2/4 ♪ ♩ ♪; (3) tied to the next full beat: 2/4 ♫♫⌐♩; (4) or tied to more than a full beat: 2/4 ♫ ♫⌐♩ .

Syncopated accents are emphasized if the normal metric accent is used in an accompaniment.

Ex. 19f.   Clap the rhythms in Fig. 51, counting the beat-numbers and

the "ands" of the half-beats. Do not drag the beats on the syncopations. Sing the rhythms with *la*.

Fig. 51

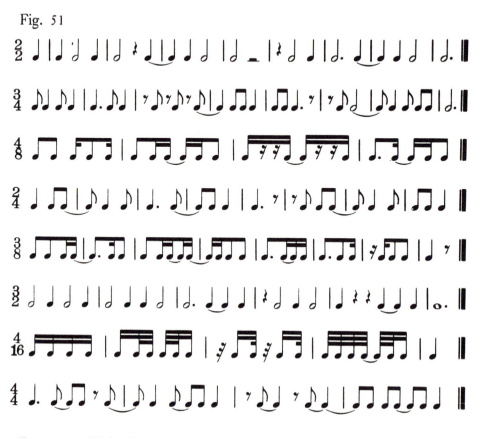

Ex. 19g.   Write four-measure units from each line of Fig. 51 from
memory.

Half-beat Values in Mixed Meters

Unless otherwise specified, an eighth note in $\frac{3\text{-}4}{8}$ meter is equal to
a *half* beat of $\frac{2\text{-}3\text{-}4}{4}$; a sixteenth note in $\frac{3\text{-}4}{16}$ equals a half beat of $\frac{3\text{-}4}{8}$. The
same relationship holds for $\frac{2\text{-}3\text{-}4}{2}$ and $\frac{2\text{-}3\text{-}4}{4}$; for example, measure 2 in
the first line of Fig. 52 may be counted as 1 plus 2 "ands."

Ex. 19h.   Clap the rhythms of Fig. 52, then sing with *la*.

Fig. 52

Metric changes in some melodies have different beat units; specifically indicated ♩ = ♪, the beat unit of 4/4 equals that of 3/8.

Ex. 19i. Clap the rhythms of Fig. 53, giving equal time to every one-beat note and rest.

Fig. 53

Ex. 19j. Read the notes of the melodies of Section 2 by scale step numbers without singing them. Try to develop facility in reading them quickly, then sing the melodies.

Major: Simple Meter, Half and Beat-and-a-half Values

5   TENDERLY   DOWLAND

6   SCHERZANDO   ESTHONIA

7   MAESTOSO   C. GOLDMARK

8   LIGHTLY   ENGLAND

9   ZART   SILCHER

10   TRANQUILLY   DUNSTABLE

15 ENERGETIC AND STRONGLY ACCENTED   ENGLAND

16 LUSTIG   GERMANY

17 ANDANTE SOSTENUTO   SALIERI

18 ALLEGRO   LORTZING

19 VIGOROUSLY   SCOTLAND

26 QUIETLY UNITED STATES

27 ANDANTE TYROL

28 MODERATO

UNITED STATES

29 ALLEGRETTO von FLOTOW

30 FRÖHLICH FINE GERMANY

31 MODÉRÉ FRANCE

D. C. AL FINE

66 SECTION 2

38 AFFETTUOSO   DONIZETTI

39 LARGAMENTE   GERMANY

40 VIVO   SPAIN

Syncopation

41 MODERATO   HANDEL

42 VIVACE   CROATIA

43   ALLEGRO   VERDI

44   SLOWLY, WITH DEEP FEELING   NEGRO SPIRITUAL

45   FEURIG   CZECHOSLOVAKIA

46   LANGSAM   GERMANY

47   VIGOROSO   CZECHOSLOVAKIA

48   SLOWLY   SPIRITUAL

49 SCHERZANDO   SAINT-SAENS

50 VIGOROUSLY   WALES

51 LIVELY   NEGRO SPIRITUAL

52 GRAVE   HANDEL

53 ALLEGRO CON GRAZIA   SPAIN

CHAPTER

5

The Alto Clef

THE main purpose of the great staff is to accommodate the gamut of keyboard instruments. Used singly, the G and F staves, with additional ledger lines, accommodate the range of solo voice parts and music for solo instruments. To reduce the number of ledger lines required, however, composers in the past used the device of a third clef, the C clef. The pitch of C was located on whichever line of the staff was most convenient for notating music in the normal ranges of baritone, tenor, alto, mezzo soprano, and soprano voices or instruments. Only the alto and tenor C clefs are still being used; the rest are obsolete. The alto clef is used in music for the viola; the tenor clef is used in music for cello, bassoon, and tenor trombone. A reading knowledge of these two clefs is necessary to understand and play chamber and orchestral music.

Fig. 54

Our present concern is with the alto clef, shown in Fig. 54. Middle C is on the center line. The two lower lines of the treble and the two upper lines of the bass staves make up the rest of the alto staff.

Ex. 20a.   Memorize the lines and spaces of the alto staff.

Ex. 20b.   Read the letter names of the notes written on the alto staff in Section 3.

Alto Clef Transposition

The alto clef can be used to *transpose* (shift) a melody from its original key into the key with the next higher letter by substituting the alto clef for the G clef. For example, a melody in C or C♯ can be read in D, D♭, or E♭ (D♯).

Proceed as follows: Write out a number of alto clef signatures in

70

each key, following Fig. 55. If a melody is in G or G♭, take the alto clef signature for A or A♭ and cover the original key signature. Read the notes in the new key.

Fig. 55

Ex. 20c.   Transpose melodies in the treble clef in Section 3 in the manner described, reading the notes by letter name.

Melodies in the bass clef may be transposed in the same manner from the original key to keys with the next lower letter: for example from C♯ or C to B or B♭.

Ex. 20d.   Transpose melodies in the bass clef in Section 3 in the manner described above.

Quarter-beat Values in Simple Meter

A beat unit may be divided into quarter-of-a-beat values:

Beat-unit /2: Quarter-beat values ♩♩♩♩; quarter-beat rests ♩ 𝄾 ♩ 𝄾
          /4: Quarter-beat values ♫♫♫♫; quarter-beat rests ♫ 𝄿 ♪ 𝄿
          /8: Quarter-beat values ♬♬♬♬; quarter-beat rests ♬ 𝄿 ♬ 𝄿

Quarter-beat values are combined in various ways. Using the quarter note as beat unit, here are the combinations: ♬♬ = ♪♬; ♬♬ = ♫♪; ♬♬ = ♪♩. ; ♬♬ = ♫♩

Ex. 21a.   Write the same combinations using half, eighth, and sixteenth notes as beat units.

Ex. 21b.   Practice clapping these combinations. One way is to count the divisions as if the meter in /4 were in /16, so that it amounts to four quick subbeats. Another method of counting is

1- ta- and- ta

or 1- a - and- a.

After you have gotten the feel of the time relationships, drop the split-beat counting.

Ex. 21c.   Clap the following rhythms, letting your eyes travel ahead. *Don't guess the rhythm.* You must know where each beat begins and how it is divided.

Fig. 56

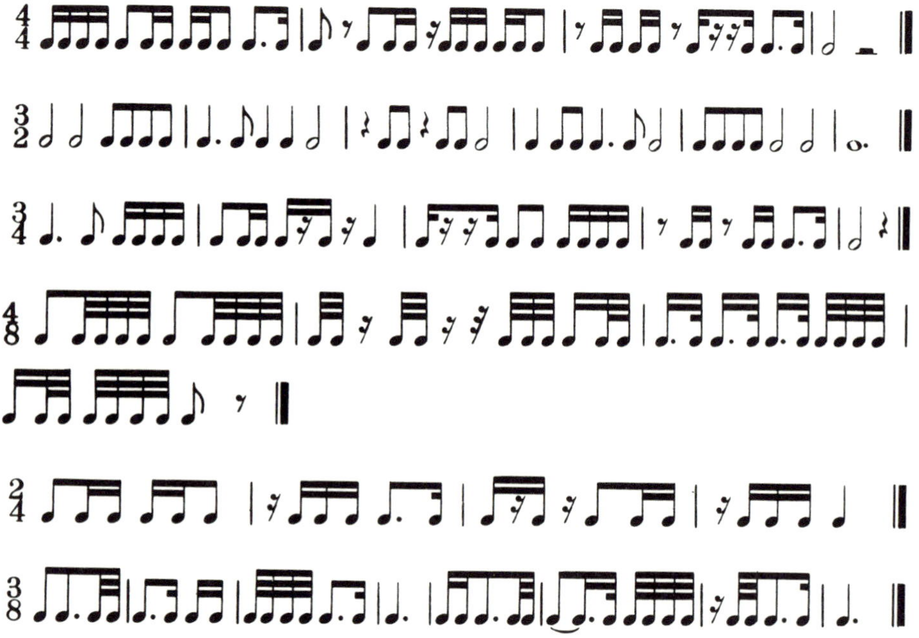

Ex. 21d.   Read four-measure units in each line of Ex. 21c silently, then write them down from memory.

Ex. 21e.   Combine two-measure units in 4/16 of Exs. 3b, 12b, 15d, 15g, and 17a to make single measures in 2/4. Clap and count as in Ex. 21b.

Quarter-beat Values in Syncopation

Ex. 21f.   Clap the rhythms in Fig. 57, then sing with *la*, without breaking the regularity of the beats.

Fig. 57

Ex. 21g. Read two-measure units of Fig. 57, then write each unit down from memory.

The Double-Dotted Note as Quarter-of-a-beat Value

The rhythm value of the note in brackets is a quarter-of-a-beat value:

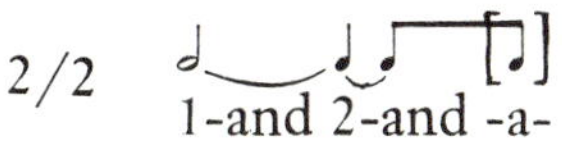

2/2   1-and 2-and -a-

It is represented also as: ♩.(.), that is, as a double-dotted note. The first dot has half the value of the note; the second dot has half the value of the first dot. Similarly, 2/4 ♩.. ♪ equals 1 and 2- and- a

Ex. 21h. Clap the rhythms in Fig. 58, then sing with *la*.

Fig. 58

Ex. 21i. Read the notes of the melodies of Section 3 by scale step numbers without singing them. Try to develop facility in reading them quickly, then sing the melodies.

Simple Meter: the Beat Divided in Quarters

74

6 ANDANTE CON MOTO ⌐1⌐ ⌐2⌐ ITALY

7 ANDANTE ESPRESSIVO GRETRY

8 ALLEGRETTO CIMAROSA

9 MAESTOSO HANDEL

76 SECTION 3

10 ALLEGRO ITALY

11 ALLEGRO PESANTE CZECHOSLOVAKIA

12 GAI LULLY

13 ANDANTE GERMANY

14 ALLEGRO BRAHMS

15 CHANTANT FRANCE

16 **ALLEGRO POMPOSO**

NORWAY

17 **SCHERZANDO**

SACCHINI

FINE

Three-voice Canon

18 **ALLEGRETTO**

WEBBE

78 SECTION 3

19 ALLEGRO SCOTLAND

20 LEGER RAMEAU

21 ALLEGRO GERMANY

22 ALLEGRO BEETHOVEN

23   ANDANTE SOSTENUTO   MONSIGNY

24   ANDANTE CANTABILE   MOZART

25   MODERATELY FAST

UNITED STATES   26   ANDANTE NON TROPPO   SALIERI

IV

27   MODERATO   SPAIN

FINE

dal Seg.
al Fine

28 GAI   FRANCE

mf

1 | 2

29 ZIEMLICH LANGSAM   SCHUBERT

pp

mf

30 ALLEGRO MARZIALE   HALEVY

mf

1 | 2   31 SCHERZOSO   SACCHINI

f   *p*

II   *mf*

1 | 2   32 ALLEGRETTO   VON WEBER

dim.   *mp*

V7

33   ALLEGRO NON TROPPO   OFFENBACH

34   RISOLUTO   HANDEL

35   ANDANTE   SWEDEN

36   LARGO   SALIERI

37   ALLEGRETTO   HAYDN

II

38   ANDANTINO   MONSIGNY

Seq.   II

39   ANDANTE   RAMEAU

II   rall.

40   MÄSSIG   VON WEBER

41   SCHERZANDO   BELLINI

42   ANDANTE   MOZART

43   LEBHAFT   ROUMANIA

44   ALLEGRO   SWEDEN

45   WITH ABANDON   CZECHOSLOVAKIA

46 ALLEGRO

ENGLAND

mf

III

47 MARZIALE

MOZART

f

mf

cresc.   poco   a   poco

48 LIVELY

UNITED STATES

mf

VI

49 ALLEGRETTO

BRAHMS

50 ANDANTE CANTABILE

SALIERI

51 LEGER

FRANCE

52 ALLEGRETTO GRAZIOSO, LEGGIERO

SCARLATTI

53 SPIRITED

COPLAND

54   MODÉRÉ DECIDÉ   GRETRY

55   ALLEGRETTO   MEXICO

56   MÄSSIG   SCHUBERT

57   LUSTIG   MAHLER

Syncopation

58 FAST — WALES

59 TENDERLY — THOMPSON

60 SLOWLY — NEGRO SPIRITUAL

61 MODERATO — IRELAND

62 VIGOROUSLY NEGRO SPIRITUAL

mf

1 | 2 | 63 ALLEGRO PERGOLESI

mf

64 MODERATELY FAST SCOTLAND

mf *f*

65 FERVENTLY NEGRO SPIRITUAL

mf *soft*

louder *soft*

66 ANDANTE UNITED STATES

ritard. *mp*

dim. *cresc.* *mf*

p

dim. e rit.

Double-dotted Note Values

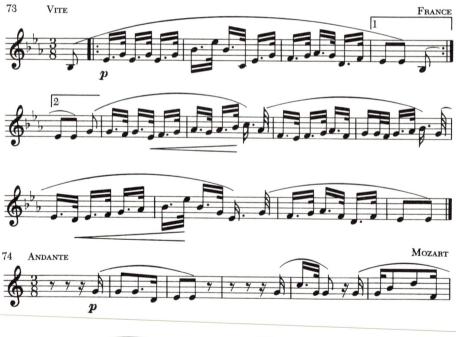

Beat Unit, an Eighth Note; Quarter-beat, a Thirty-second Note

CHAPTER

6

The Ascending Melodic Minor Scale

PLAY Fig. 59. The first eight measures of the melody (a) are clearly in the key of A major. The next four measures (b) are exactly the same except that C♮ is used instead of C♯. (The sign (♮) in measure 9 is called a *natural* sign. It is used to cancel a sharp or flat in the key signature, or to cancel a previously sharped or flatted note in the measure. Sharps or flats additional to those in the key signature, and naturals which cancel any signature flats or sharps, are called *accidentals*.)

Fig. 59

The melody tones of measures 9 to 14, arranged in scale order, A-B-C-D-E-F♯-G♯-A, form the *ascending melodic minor scale*.

The pattern of this scale, starting from A, is given in Fig. 60a. The piano keys are separated in Fig. 60b to show the half and whole step order. Observe that the scale is the same as the major scale except for scale-step 3.

Major and minor scales, like the two scales used in Fig. 59, which have the same tonic note, have a *tonic* relationship. A major is the *tonic*

Fig. 60a

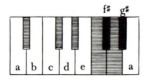

Fig. 60b

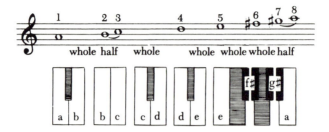

(or *parallel*) *major* scale of a minor; and a minor is the *tonic* or *parallel minor* scale of A major. Hereafter, capital letters will be used to denote major keys and small letters to denote minor keys.

Ex. 22a.   Practice singing the ascending melodic minor scale in *a*, using any octave convenient to your voice.

Ex. 22b.   Write the ascending melodic minor scale in the following keys: d, e, g, b, c, f♯, f, c♯, b♭, g♯, e♭, and d♯. Follow the pattern in Fig. 60, putting a sharp or flat before any tone which requires it. In the keys of g♯ and d♯ it will be necessary to use a double sharp, indicated by ✕, for the seventh scale step, following the rule that no letter may be omitted nor any used twice; for example, F✕-G♯, not G-G♯.

Ex. 22c.   Practice singing Ex. 4c, in the ascending melodic minor scale. Write these tones out in the keys of a, d, e, and g.

In some melodies the tones 5-6-7-8 of the ascending melodic minor are also used in the opposite direction, 8-7-6-5 or 8-7-6-7-8.

The Minor Third

The scale tones 1-3 in minor form an interval of a *minor third*. Minor-third tones are three half steps apart and encompass three letters: A-B-C.

Ex. 22d.   Name by letter a minor third up from each note in Fig. 23, then sing minor thirds up from each tone. Start practice by singing

1-2-3, 1-3 in minor. Compare these thirds with the major; sing a major, then a minor third from each tone.

Ex. 22e.   Name by letter a minor third down from each note in Fig. 23, then sing minor thirds down from each tone. Start practice by singing 3-2-1, 3-1 in minor. If you experience difficulty with this, sing a minor second, 3-2, then a major second, 2-1. Sing major, then minor, thirds down alternately from each note in Fig. 23.

The I, V, and V⁷ Chords in Minor

The tonic chord in minor differs from the major tonic because of the minor third scale step, A-[C]-E in *a* minor. Minor triads have a minor third from root to chord third.

Ex. 23a.   Write the minor I chord for each key listed in Ex. 22b in the treble, bass, and alto staves.

Ex. 23b.   Change every E to E♭ in Ex. 7b, then practice singing this exercise in c minor.

The tones of V and V⁷ are the same in major and minor.

Ex. 23c.   Practice Ex. 7i in minor. Do the same with Ex. 18b.

Ex. 23d.   Write out Ex. 23c in a, d, e, and g.

Minor Triads in Major Keys

In major, triads formed on scale step 2 (2-4-6), on 6 ($\overline{6}$-1-3), and on 3 (3-5-7) are minor-sounding triads which are used in contrast to, or as occasional substitutes for, the major triads, I, IV, and V.

Ex. 24a.   Considering each note in Fig. 23 as tonic, write out the II triad of each major key.

Ex. 24b.   Sing the following tones in major, in the progression IV-II: 8-6-4, 6-4-2, 5; 1-4-6, 6-4-2, 5; 5, 6-4-1, 2-4-6, 5; 3, 4-6-8, 4-6-$\underline{2}$, 7; in the progression II-V and V⁷: 3, 4-6-$\underline{2}$, 5-7-$\underline{2}$, 8; 5, 6-2-4, 2-$\overline{7}$-5, 1; 3, 4-6-2, 4-5-$\overline{7}$, 1; 3, 2-4-6, 5-4-$\overline{7}$, 1; 8, $\underline{2}$-6-4, 7-5-4, 3.

Ex. 24c.   Considering each note of Fig. 23 as tonic, write out the VI triad in each major key.

Ex. 24d.   Sing the following tones in the progression VI-II: $\overline{5}$,$\overline{6}$-1-3, 2-4-6, 5; 1-$\overline{6}$-3, 4-2-6, 5; 8-6-3, 2-6-4, $\overline{7}$; in VI-IV: 8-6-3, 4-6-8, 7;

3-8-6, 8-6-4, 5; 5, 6-3-1, 4-1-$\bar{6}$, $\bar{7}$; in VI-V and V⁷: 3-8-6, 7-5-2, 8; 3-6-8, 7-2-5, 8; 5, 6-8-3, 4-2-$\bar{7}$-$\bar{5}$, 1.

Ex. 24e. Considering each note of Fig. 23 as tonic, write out the III chord in each major key.

Ex. 24f. Sing the following major scale tones in the progression, III-IV: 8, 7-5-3-7, 6-4-1-6, 5; 8, 7-3-5-7, 6-1-4-6, 2; In III-VI: 8, 7-5-3-7, 8-6-3, 2.

Ex. 24g. Write out Exs. 24b, d, and f in C and other major keys; sing the notes.

The Descending Melodic Minor Scale

Sing the tones, 5-4-3-2 in minor. Four-tone scale series are called *tetrachords*. Repeat the tones several times, using *la*. Then call the same tones 8-7-6-5. The minor scale tones 5-4-3-2 sound like 8-7-6-5 of the *descending melodic minor scale*, Fig. 61a. The first five tones of the melodic minor scale ascending and descending are the same, but there is a difference between the two in their sixth and seventh scale steps. The pattern of half and whole steps for the descending melodic minor is given in Fig. 61b. Compare this with Fig. 60b.

Fig. 61a

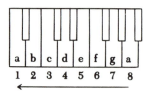

Fig. 61b

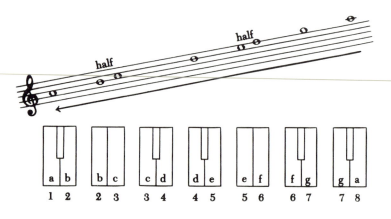

Ex. 25a. Practice singing the descending melodic minor scale in a, using any octave convenient to your vocal range.

Ex. 25b. Write the melodic minor descending in the keys listed in Ex. 22b, inserting the accidentals required for the tones of each scale.

Ex. 25c. Practice singing these scale steps in the descending melodic minor: 8-7-6-5; 8-5-8-7-6-5; 8-7-6-7-6-5; 8-5-6-7-6-5.

Ex. 25d. Practice singing up and down the melodic minor scale in ascending and descending form.

The Aeolian Mode

Try singing up along the descending form of the melodic minor scale: A-B-C-D-E-F-G-A. This series of tones roughly corresponds to an old ecclesiastical scale called the *Aeolian mode*, sometimes called the *Hypodorian* mode, a scale originally derived from ancient Greek music. In Western European music this scale became known as the *pure* or *natural* minor scale. Many folk melodies derive their tones from this scale.

The term *mode* initially referred to the style or manner in which ecclesiastical melodies were sung, incidentally involving the use of tones which centered to a degree around a certain "final" note. The term *mode* is also used to distinguish the major or minor phase of a tonality. We speak of the *major* mode of C and the *minor* mode of c.

Turn back to Fig. 59. You will observe that the melody momentarily shifts from the scale tones of a to tones of C at (c) and (d). This may not be readily apparent since the tones of a natural minor are the same as those of C. The important difference is that the tone A is the tonal center of a minor and the tone C is the tonal center of C major.

Relative Keys

Paired major and minor keys, such as C and a, are called *relative* keys. The key of a is the *relative minor* of C; conversely C is the *relative major* of a. Relative keys share the same key signature; C major and a minor therefore have the same signature. Note that the tone A is the sixth scale step of C. The sixth scale step of any major key is the tonic tone of its relative minor; the sixth scale step is also three steps down from the major tonic tone. This is an easy way to locate the tonic of the relative minor.

Ex. 26a. Find the tonic tone of the relative minor for each of the following major keys: G, F, D, B♭, A, E♭, A♭, B, D♭, F♯, G♭, C♯, C♭.

The third scale step of any minor key is the tonic tone of its relative major.

Ex. 26b.   Find the tonic tone of the relative major keys from each of the minor keys listed in Ex. 22b.

Compare the C major scale with the ascending melodic minor scale of a, in Fig. 60b. The latter has F♯ and G♯ as scale steps six and seven. Since a minor has the same signature as C major, these two sharps must be written in for each F and G, when writing the ascending melodic a minor scale.

Ex. 26c.   Write the key signature of each minor key listed in Ex. 22b, followed by the upper tetrachord (5-6-7-8) of the ascending melodic minor scale in each key. Remember to raise the sixth and seventh scale steps. When the key signature has a flat for step six and/or step

Fig. 62

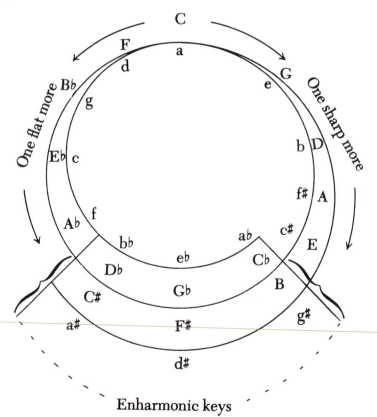

Enharmonic keys

seven, use a natural sign to raise the note (or notes); tones 6 and 7, which are natural in the signature, become sharped; leading tones which are sharped become double-sharped.

Ex. 26d.   Write the descending upper tetrachord (8-7-6-5) of each melodic minor scale. The notes of the descending tetrachord 8-7-6-5 conform to the key signature. When used in the same measure with the ascending tetrachord, cancel the sharps or flat the notes accordingly.

Relative major-minor keys are diagrammed in Fig. 62. Keys which look the same on the piano keyboard, but which are written differently—for example, C♯ and D♭ or a♯ and b♭—are called *enharmonic keys*. These also are indicated in Fig. 62.

Ex. 26e.   Memorize the related keys shown in Fig. 62.

Recognizing the Minor in Melody

Students frequently assume that a given key signature automatically means a major key. This error can be overcome by making a habit of scanning the melody. Look at the *last* melody tone. It is almost invariably the tonic. Is it the major or relative minor tonic? Look at the beginning tones. Melodies in major rarely begin on scale step six, and such a beginning indicates the minor. Look for raised scale tones. Are they the raised six and seven of the melodic minor? Look for chord skips. Do you find skips along I and/or V (V⁷) of the major? In C, these would be C-E-G; G-B-D-(F); in a minor, A-C-E; E-G♯-B-(D).

Many short melodies which start in major continue to the end in the same key. Others start in major, shift to the relative minor, without a change of key signature, and then return to close in the original key. Sometimes minor melodies shift to the relative major and then return and close in the original minor key. The student must learn to recognize such key changes.

Composers use the minor mode in this kind of key change for the sake of variety. A theme originally announced in major may appear immediately or later in minor, as in Fig. 59; variety is provided by the change in mode, and unity by the resemblance of the major and minor versions. Also, in an A-B-A form, the contrast between the A and B sections is heightened if they are in different modes. The emotions projected by the minor mode are introspection, sadness, melancholy, grief, despair, and tragedy.

Ex. 26f.   Read the notes of the melodies of Section 4 by scale step numbers without singing them. Try to develop facility in reading them quickly, then sing the melodies.

SECTION 4

Scale Step 3 in Minor, Simple Meters

98

8 MODERATO   FRANCE

9 DOLCE   SWEDEN

10 ANIMATO   FRANCE

11 ANDANTE, TENERAMENTE   SPAIN

12 ALLEGRETTO RAMEAU

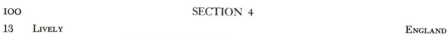

13 LIVELY ENGLAND

14 MARCATO SWEDEN

15 VIF FRANCE

16 ALLEGRETTO SPAIN

The Melodic Minor, Simple Meters

17 VIVACE SCHUMANN

18   DOLENTE   SPAIN

con calore   *rit.*

19   SCHERZANDO   ITALY

p

dim.   *mf*

20   MODERATO   NORWAY

mp

mf   *dim.*   *p*

RAMEAU

21   LEGER   1.   2.

pp   *cedez*

22   SLOWLY   UNITED STATES

p   *mf*

23   VIGOROUSLY   WALES

mf   I   V   *rit.*   *p*   *mf*

dim.   FINE *f*

24 ANDANTINO   COUPERIN

25 VIVO   FINLAND

26 AMOROSO   SPAIN

27 RISOLUTO   ITALY

28 VIGOUREAUX   FRANCE

29 FOUR-VOICE CANON GOUNOD

30 MODERATO WALES

31 ANDANTINO VON WEBER

32 TRANQUILLO SPAIN

33 MÄCHTIG HANDEL

34 TRISTE SPAIN

35   **LARGHETTO**   **LULLY**

36 **ALLEGRO**   **WILSON**

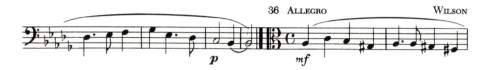

37   **ALLEGRETTO**   **GLUCK**

38   **VIF**   **LECOCQ**

39   **ANDANTINO**   **AUBER**

40   **VIGOROSO**   **VIOTTI**

41 VIVACE   HUNGARY

mp   mf

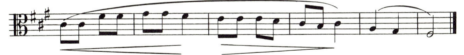

42 BROADLY   THOMPSON

f

IV   dim.   mp

43 SLOWLY   NEGRO SPIRITUAL

p   mf

44 GRACIEUX   SAINT SAËNS

mf

dim.   poco   a   poco   p

mf   dim.   poco   a   poco   p

45 ALLEGRO   RAMEAU

mf

mp   mf

46 A PIACERE — SPAIN

47 ALLEGRETTO — J. S. BACH

48 ANDANTINO CANTABILE — BIZET

49 LARGHETTO HANDEL

50 LEGGIERO GLUCK

51 ANDANTE SOSPIRANDO TCHAIKOWSKY

52 LARGO SAINT-SAËNS

CHAPTER
7

The Beat-unit Divided in Thirds, in Simple Meter

THREE tones equal in value may occupy a beat. Since there is no note-symbol indicating a third-of-a-beat value, a makeshift is used. Three notes are grouped together by a curved line or bracket which encloses a small figure 3, over or under the group ♩♩♩ * This three-note group is called a *triplet*. Each note of the triplet equals a third-of-a-beat.**

The one-beat triplet is written in note values which are the next value *below* the beat-unit; see Fig. 63.

Fig. 63

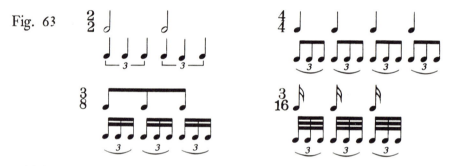

Triplet tones, unless otherwise indicated, must be equal in duration. As a preliminary exercise, clap 3/8 ♩. | ♩. | ♩♩♩ | ♩. ||. Keeping the same rhythmic proportions, substitute single beats for each pair of measures, thus: 3/8 ♩. ♩. | ♩♩♩ ♩. ||. The same time relationship holds for 2/4 𝄽 𝄽 | 𝄽𝄽 𝄽 ||.

Ex. 27a.   Clap the rhythms in Fig. 64, then sing with *la*. Do not stretch the beat out for the triplets, nor shorten the beat on full-beat values. When a series of triplets occurs, the curved line and the number 3 are discontinued after the first few, since the pattern is clear.

Ex. 27b.   Read each line of Fig. 64 silently, then write it down from memory.

---

* A bracket is used to enclose a triplet made up of notes not connected by beams. A curved line encloses a triplet of beamed notes. Do not confuse the curved line with either the tie or the slur. The tie always joins adjacent notes of the same pitch. The slur encloses different notes as a phrasing device.

** Triplets other than those of one-beat value will be studied later.

Fig. 64

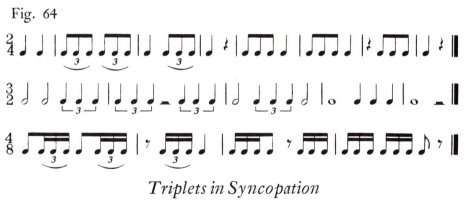

Triplets in Syncopation

A tie from the last note of a triplet to the beginning of the next beat, or a note on the last beat tied over the bar line to the first note of a triplet, sets up a syncopated rhythm.

Ex. 27c.   Practice the rhythms of Fig. 65 as directed in Exs. 27a and 27b.

Fig. 65

Third-of-a-beat notes may be combined in the proportion of two-thirds to one-third. The triplet then appears as 2/2 ♩ ♩♩ ♩; 3/4 ♩ ♪ ♩ ♪ ♩ ♪; and 4/8 ♫ ♫ ♫ ♫. In a one-third to two-thirds proportion, the beat is syncopated. Rests may occupy any portion of the triplet.

Ex. 27d.   Clap the rhythms of Fig. 66, then sing with *la*.

Ex. 27e.   Write four-measure units from each line of Fig. 66 from memory.

Fig. 66

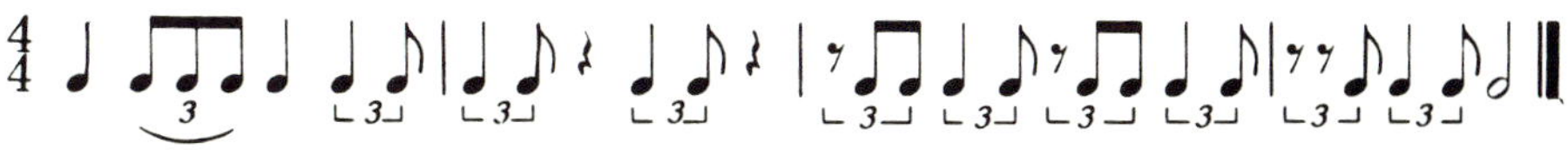

The Harmonic Minor Scale

Sing up the scale described as the Aeolian mode or natural minor, Fig. 61. Repeat this, substituting G♯ for G. The scale so altered is the *harmonic minor scale*, shown in Fig. 67. This scale has the same form ascending and descending. Both the harmonic and the melodic minor, ascending or descending, may appear in the same minor melody.

Fig. 67

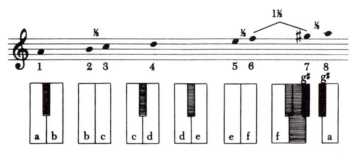

The pattern for the harmonic minor scale is:

1	2	3	4	5	6	7	8
whole step	half step	whole step	whole step	half step	whole step plus half step	half step	

The interval 6-7 (F-G♯) is a half-step larger than a major second, and is called an *augmented second*. In size it is equivalent to a minor third. Equivalent intervals are called *enharmonic intervals*.

Ex. 28a. Practice singing the harmonic minor scale in any octave convenient to your voice.

Ex. 28b. Write out the harmonic minor scale from each tonic listed in Ex. 22b, inserting the necessary accidentals for each tone.

Ex. 28c. Write the key signature for each of these keys, then write the upper tetrachord of the harmonic minor in each key, inserting the required accidentals.

Ex. 28d. Practice singing Exs. 4f, 7a, 13b, 24b, 24d, 24f, and 25c in the harmonic minor tones.

The harmonic minor, centering around scale step 5, is the scale basis for some types of Spanish and Latin American folk melodies which may also include the upper tetrachord of the descending melodic minor.

Ex. 28e. Practice singing the following in the harmonic scale: $\overline{5}$-$\overline{5}$-$\overline{5}$-$\overline{6}$-$\overline{7}$-1-2-3-4-5-4-3-2-1; $\overline{7}\flat$-$\overline{6}\flat$-$\overline{5}$-$\overline{4}$-$\overline{5}$ (melodic minor).

The Minor Sixth

The minor sixth is a semitone smaller than the major sixth. Sing the scale tones $\overline{5}$-1, 1-3, $\overline{5}$-3 in minor. The skip $\overline{5}$-3 in minor is a minor sixth. These tones are a perfect fifth plus a semitone apart, and encompass six letters; in a, they are E-F♯-G♯-A-B-C. Common skips of a minor sixth in minor are: $\overline{5}$-3, 1-6 (harmonic minor), and $\overline{7}$-5; in major, 3-8, $\overline{6}$-4, and $\overline{7}$-5.

Ex. 29a. Name by letter a minor sixth up from each note in Fig. 23, then sing minor sixths up from each tone. Start by practicing $\overline{5}$-1, 1-3, $\overline{5}$-3 in minor.

Ex. 29b. Name by letter a minor sixth down from each note in Fig. 23, then sing minor sixths down from each tone. Start by review practice of minor thirds down; then sing 3-1, 1-$\overline{5}$, 3-$\overline{5}$.

The IV Chord in Minor

The IV in minor, 4-6♭ (lowered)-8 is a minor-sounding triad; in the key of a, it is D-F-A.

Ex. 30a. Write the IV chord of each key listed in Ex. 22b.

Ex. 30b. Review Ex. 13b, singing the chord tones in minor.

The II Chord in Minor; the VII Triad

Play the tones B-D-F. These form the II triad in a minor. The minor II chord is a *diminished triad*, so called because the interval from root to fifth is a *diminished fifth*, which is a semitone smaller than a perfect fifth. The same tones in C major form the VII triad. The tones G♯-B-D form the VII triad in a minor. The II in minor and the VII in major and minor, then, are diminished triads.

Ex. 30c.   Write the II chord from each key listed in Ex. 22b.

Ex. 30d.   Review Ex. 24b, singing the tones in minor.

Ex. 30e.   Write the VII triad from each key listed in Ex. 26a.

Ex. 30f.   Practice singing the tones of the VII triad: 1, $\overline{7}$-2-4, 3; 3, 4-2-$\overline{7}$, 1; 3, 2-4-$\overline{7}$, 1; 1, $\overline{7}$-4-2, 3; 1, 2-$\overline{7}$-4, 3.

Ex. 30g.   Write out the notes in Exs. 24b, 24d, and 24f in c (harmonic) minor, and in other minor keys; sing from your notes. Write out Ex. 30f in c minor and other minor keys; sing the notes.

The Diminished Fifth; the Augmented Fourth

Scale steps $\overline{7}$-4 in major and minor, and scale steps 2-6 in the harmonic minor, form an interval of a diminished fifth. The diminished fifth encompasses five letters, B-C-D-E-F. The same scale tones inverted—4-7 (F-G-A-B)—form an interval of an *augmented fourth*, which is a semitone larger than a perfect fourth. The diminished fifth and the augmented fourth, as intervals, sound the same. These intervals are further examples of enharmonic intervals. In both, the tones are separated by three whole tones. The interval of the augmented fourth-diminished fifth is therefore referred to as a *tritone*.

Ex. 31a.   Name by letter a diminished fifth up from each note in Fig. 23, then sing diminished fifths up from each tone. Practice by singing $\overline{7}$-4; then sing both tones with *la*.

Ex. 31b.   Name by letter an augmented fourth up from each note in Fig. 23. Bear in mind that although the tones on the piano $\overline{B}$-F and $\overline{B}$-E♯ are the same, the latter is an augmented fourth.

Ex. 31c.   Name by letter a diminished fifth down from each note in Fig. 23, then sing diminished fifths down from each tone. Practice by singing 4-$\overline{7}$; then sing the same tones with *la*.

Compound Meters

We have seen that two measures of simple duple meter joined—2/4 plus 2/4—form a single measure of simple quadruple meter, 4/4. In similar fashion two measures of simple triple meter, 3/4 plus 3/4, form a single measure of six beats or *sextuple meter*:

In 3/4 meter the normal accent falls on beat one of each measure. In 6/4 the beats group themselves into two units, each with three beats: ♩ ♩ ♩ ♩ ♩ ♩, so that the feeling in sextuple meter is one of two large beats 1   2 to a measure, each large beat composed of a main beat and two subbeats: 1 2 3 4 5 6 ♩ ♩ ♩ ♩ ♩ ♩ Each main beat plus the subbeats form a *superbeat*. The meter 1   2 signature for 6/4 might therefore be written as 2 beats in a measure, with a superbeat unit of ♩ ♩ ♩ or ♩.

In a slow tempo the main and subbeats in sextuple meter are sensed as single, individual beats, but this is far less common than hearing sextuple meter as 2 main beats plus subbeats.

Any meter in which the beat unit is a composite of a main beat and two subbeats is called a *compound meter*. Sextuple meter should therefore be regarded as *compound duple meter*.

Now compare the rhythm in the following meters:

2/4
6/8

Music in 2/4 with a rhythm of continuous triplets cannot be distinguished by the ear from 6/8 meter. Composers therefore use sextuple meter when the beat is *consistently* divided in three; they use

Fig. 68

meters like 2/4 when the beat is mainly divided in two, four, or eight parts, with perhaps occasional triplets.

In the following exercises think of 6/2 as 2/𝅗𝅥·; 6/4 as 2/𝅘𝅥.; 6/8 as 2/𝅘𝅥. and 6/16 as 2/♪. In other words, think of the beat as 2/ and the beat unit as a group of three ♫♩ or as a dotted note: 𝅘𝅥.; 𝅘𝅥 𝅘𝅥 𝅘𝅥 or 𝅗𝅥.; 𝅗𝅥 𝅗𝅥 𝅗𝅥 or 𝅝·

Ex. 32a.   Clap the rhythms in Fig. 68, then sing with *la*.

Ex. 32b.   Read four-measure units of each line of Fig. 68 silently, then write each unit from memory.

Nonetuple Meter

Nonetuple meter—nine beats—is a *compound triple meter* of three main beats, each with two subbeats, to a measure: 1̲ 2̲ 3̲ 4̲ 5̲ 6̲ 7̲ 8̲ 9̲. The beat unit, as in sextuple meter, is a dotted note representing a group of three beats, thus: 9/4 = 3/𝅗𝅥. ; 9/8 = 3/𝅘𝅥. ; 9/16 = 3/♪. Think of the meter as 3; and each beat unit as a group of three notes or as a dotted note.

Ex. 32c.   Clap the rhythms in Fig. 69 then sing with *la*.

Fig. 69

Ex. 32d.   Write each line of Fig. 69 from memory.

Duodecuple Meter

Duodecuple meter, twelve beats, is *compound quadruple meter*, consisting of four main beats, each with two subbeats, to a measure: 1̲ 2̲ 3̲ 4̲ 5̲ 6̲ 7̲ 8̲ 9̲ 10̲ 11̲ 12. The beats, as in sextuple and nonetuple meters, are grouped in threes; and the beat unit is a dotted note. 12/4 = 4/𝅗𝅥. ; 12/8 = 4/𝅘𝅥. ; 12/16 = 4/♪. Think of the meter as being in 4/ and the beat unit as being a group of three or a dotted note.

Ex. 32e.   Clap the rhythms in Fig. 70, then sing with *la*.

Fig. 70

Composers occasionally use a conventional simple triple meter when the music is actually compound duple. Notice how it feels more natural to count this *Faust Waltz* in two rather than in three.

Fig. 71

Ex. 32f.   Revise Ex. 27a, Fig. 64, changing simple duple, triple, and quadruple meters to compound meters by changing simple beat units to dotted notes and removing triplet symbols; then sing with *la*.

Ex. 32g.   Read the notes of the melodies of Section 5 by scale step number without singing them. Try to develop facility in reading them quickly.

SECTION 5

The One-beat Triplet in Simple Meters

1 ANIMATO — SPAIN

2 LEGER — FRANCE

3 ALLEGRO, MARZIALE — BOIELDIEU

4 MODERE — FRANCE

5 GAILY — UNITED STATES

6 LUSTIG SCHUMANN

7 AFFETTUOSO SPAIN

8 ANDANTE, BEN TENUTO GRIEG

9 ANDANTE, AMABILE SPAIN

10 ALLEGRO, VIGOROSO

VERDI

15   ALLEGRO, CON BRIO   PERGOLESI

Compound Meter: Undivided Subbeats

16   GRAZIOSO   MEXICO

17   ANDANTE   J. S. BACH

18   FROHLICH   CROATIA

19   LEBENDIG   GERMANY

20 ZIEMLICH LEBHAFT SCHUBERT

21 VIF FRANCE

22 MASSIG SCHULTZ

VI

23 MODERATELY FAST ENGLAND

24 ANDANTE, CANTABILE DONIZETTI

25 LARGE — RAMEAU

26 NICHT ZU GESCHWIND — SCHUBERT

27 GAI — LECOCQ

28 ANDANTE — MENDELSSOHN

29 ALLEGRETTO — FRANCE

30   ALLEGRO, GRACIOSO   GRETRY

31   ANDANTINO   GLUCK

32   LEBENDIG   SCHULTZ

33   MÄSSIG   GERMANY

34   ANDANTE   BRAHMS

35 Andante sostenuto — Beethoven

36 Moderately fast — England

37 Langsam — Germany

38 Larghetto — Gounod

SECTION 5

39   ALLEGRETTO   GOLDMARK

mp

40   MODERATO   HANDEL

mp

mf   *dim.*   *p*

VII

f   *mf*

dim.

41   LANGSAM, FEIERLICH

mf   *f*

SCHUBERT

f

42   ALLEGRO, FIERAMENTE   BERLIOZ

f

43 MODERATO   ANON.

44 FROHLICH KULLAK

45 LANGSAM SCHUMANN

46 VIVACE MOZART

47 MODERE — GOUNOD

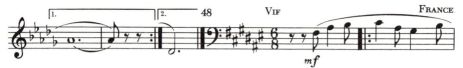

48 VIF — FRANCE

49 MAESTOSO — SMETANA

50 LEGER — MESSAGER

II

cresc.

f

51   ALLEGRETTO   BIZET

mp

mf

52   ANDANTE ESPRESSIVO   DONIZETTI

p   mp   dim.

mf   cresc.   f   dim.

f

53   LEBHAFT   OFFENBACH

p

p   p

54   MODERE   RAMEAU

mp   p   p

mp

mf   p

55 Quasi allegretto Mendelssohn

II

56 Andantino Massenet

57 Andante United States

D. C. al Fine

Minor, Compound Meter

58 Andantino France

59 Scherzando Italy

60 DOLENTE FRANCE

61 KLAGEND REICHERT

62 MODERE FRANCE

Mixed and Alternating Meters

63 LENTO LEROUX

64 LANGSAM   BRAHMS

65 MODERATO   GOUNOD

Syncopation

66 ALLEGRO   MEXICO

67 ALLEGRO   BEETHOVEN

68 AMOROSO — MEXICO

69 ANDANTE, POCO ALLEGRO — BARTOK

The Harmonic Minor

70 MOURNFULLY — UNITED STATES

71 ANDANTINO — SPAIN

72 LARGO RELIGIOSO — DURANTE

allarg.

78 CARESSANT   LE SEUR

mp

p   *rit.*

74 LENTO   GRETRY

mp   II

p

75 EXPRESSIF   PHILIDOR

mf

76 ANDANTE   MOZART

p   *cresc.*

dim.   *p*

Harmonic Minor, Scale Steps 6 and 7

Three-voice Canon

90　TRAUMERISCH　　　　　　　　　　　　　　　　HUNGARY

91　ALLEGRO, MARZIALE　　　　　　　　　　　　DENMARK

92　ANDANTE　TCHAIKOVSKY

93　VIGOROUSLY　　　　　　　　　　　　　　IRELAND

94　SCHERZANDO　　　　　　　　　　　　　　HALEVY

95 ANDANTINO   FRANCE

p

piu animato

a tempo

96 LARGE   LULLY

p

dim.

                                   97 FAST   ENGLAND

allarg.   *p*   *mf*

IV   *f*   *mf*

98 DOLENTE   MASSENET

p

cresc.   *dim.*

99   **MODERE**   **BRITTANY**

(2) *mp*

100   **LARGO**   **HANDEL**

mf   *p*   II

dim.

101 **PESANTE**   **HUNGARY**

mf

102   **ALLEGRO**   **HANDEL**

f   *mp*

cresc.   *poco*   *a*   *poco*

103   **ETWAS GESCHWIND**   **SCHUBERT**

allarg.   *f*

Minor, Variable Tones in the Upper Tetrachord

109   ANDANTE   SCHUBERT

110   ADAGIO   CROATIA

111   MODERATO   BRAHMS

112   ANDANTINO   MASSENET

CHAPTER
8

Modulation

ANY key change in the course of a piece of music is called a *modulation*. Modulations may occur anywhere in a melody; however, the change is often introduced near the cadence of a phrase or with the beginning of a new phrase. This fact underscores the importance of examining cadences in sight singing, particularly in unaccompanied melody. A key change in melody is simpler to detect when it is accompanied by chords of the new key, particularly the IV, II, V or V⁷, and I. In unaccompanied melody, clues to modulation must be discovered in the melody alone. Such clues are not always obvious in modulations to closely related keys because the new key has not more than one, two, or three tones which are different from those of the original key.

Play the melodic fragment in c minor of Fig. 72 with both given accompaniments. The first accompaniment is a modulation to f, the second to A♭. Both sound correct and point up the fact that the key of a modulation closely related to the original key is not always self-evident in unaccompanied melody. This melody may be sung with scale-step numbers in either key. The skip of a fourth in measure three (root and fifth of V) would make f the more likely key.

Fig. 72

Rubinstein

Near-related Keys

A *near-related* key is one, major or minor, which is different in signature from the original key by *one* sharp or flat, except for the relative

major or minor key. The near-related keys of any major key are:
1) the relative minor; 2) the dominant key; 3) the relative minor of
the dominant key; 4) the subdominant key; 5) the relative minor of
the subdominant key. Fig. 73 gives the scales of the near-related keys
of C major.

Fig. 73

Notice that most of the tones in keys near-related to C are the same
as the tones of C major. Apart from a different tonic tone, G major has
only one different tone, F♯. The arrows in Fig. 73 indicate tones in
related keys which are different from C major scale tones.

An easy way to remember near-related keys is: scale steps 2, 3, 4, 5,
and 6 of the original key are tonic tones of the related keys; scale steps 4
and 5 are tonics of *major* keys; scale steps 2, 3, and 6 are tonics of
minor keys.

Ex. 33a.   Write out the five near-related keys to every key listed in
Ex. 26a. Check your results with Fig. 74.

Modulations to a near-related key may occur without an accidental
in the melody: that is, a melody may modulate from C to G without
the appearance of an F♯. Cadences on the new tonic tone furnish the
clue to such modulations. Some near-related modulations are signalized
by a sudden accidental. Some accidentals do not signify a key change;

Fig. 74

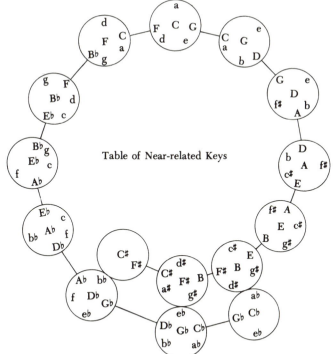

Table of Near-related Keys

they are merely incidental chromatic tones, embellishing or moving between tones of the original key.

Many tones in the original key also belong to the new key. These *common tones* or *link tones* provide a smooth transition from key to key. Common tones play a double role, since a common tone may be scale step 2 in the first key and scale step 6 in the second key.

Modulations from Major Key to All Near-Related Keys

Ex. 33b.   In the following exercises, link tones are repeated and bracketed. Write out the modulations in each unit. Sing each unit from your notes; sing the bracketed tones first with the scale number in the original key, then with the new scale number; proceed with the numbers in the new key (C to a): 8-2-7-8-7-6, 1-2-7-1; 8-5-8-7, 6-4-6-5-7, 2-1-7-1; 8-3-6-5-4-3, 5-1-6-5-4-3; 5-3-1, 5-4-3-2, 4-5-8-3-2-7-5-8; 5-3-3-5-2-2-4, 6-5-7-2-8-5-8; 1-2-3-4-2-1, 3-3-2-8-7-8-2-8. Sing these tones with *la*.

Ex. 33c.   Modulations from major key to dominant: Write out the tones and sing as in Ex. 33b (C to G): 8-5-$\underline{6\text{-}7}$, 3-5-$\overline{6}$-$\overline{7}$-1; 8-7-$\underline{6}$, 2-1-$\overline{7}$-1; 3-4-5-$\underline{8}$, 4-3-2-1; 5-6-5-$\underline{3}$, 6-7-8; 5-1-$\overline{7}$-1-$\underline{2}$, $\overline{5}$-3-4-$\overline{7}$-1; 1-3-$\underline{5}$, 8-7-$\underline{2}$-8.

Ex. 33d. Modulations from major key to the relative minor of the dominant: Write out the tones and sing as in Ex. 33b (C to e): 1-5-4-$\underline{3}$, 1-$\overline{5}$-3-2-1; 8-7-6-5-$\underline{5}$, 3-1-5-$\overline{7}$-1; 5-6-6-5-$\underline{6}$, 4-5-5-4-5-3-2-1-$\overline{7}$-1; 3-4-5-5-8-7-$\underline{8}$, 6-5-4-$\overline{7}$-1; 8-7-8-6-$\underline{7}$, 5-4-5-2-3.

Ex. 33e. Modulations from major key to subdominant: Write out the tones and sing as before (C to F): 5-5-5-3-1-$\underline{5}$, 2-3-4-3-2-1; 5-$\underline{1}$, $\overline{5}$-$\overline{7}$-2-4-3-4-2-1; 5-3-3-5-5-2-$\underline{2}$, $\overline{6}$-$\overline{5}$-1-3-4-2-$\overline{6}$-$\overline{7}$-1; 1-5-1-2-5-2-$\underline{3}$, $\overline{7}$-2-4-3-1-$\overline{5}$-1; 5-3-1-6-4-2-$\underline{4}$, 1-2-$\overline{5}$-3; 8-7-6-$\underline{6}$, 3-4-2-3.

Ex. 33f. Modulations from major key to the relative minor of the subdominant: Write out the tones and sing as before (C to d): 1-3-5-$\underline{6}$, $\overline{5}$-4-2-$\overline{7}$-1; 1-2-3-$\underline{5}$, 4-3-2-$\overline{7}$-6-5; 1-3-5-4-$\underline{3}$, 2-1-3-5-4-3; 1-$\overline{7}$-$\underline{2}$, 1-$\overline{7}$-2-3-2-1-$\overline{7}$-1; 1-1-1-$\overline{7}$-4-$\underline{4}$, 3-6-6-5-1-2-$\overline{7}$-1; 1-$\overline{7}$-$\overline{6}$-$\overline{7}$-$\underline{7}$, $\overline{6}$-$\overline{7}$-1-3-5-$\overline{7}$-1.

The foregoing exercises modulate via a *repeated* tone which is common to both keys. More often the common tone is *not repeated*. Exercises 33b to 33f should therefore be considered as preparation for Ex. 33g and Ex. 33h.

Ex. 33g. Cross out the first of the two common tones in brackets. Sing Ex. 33b to 33f slurring rapidly through the double identity of the common tone: for example, sing the first in Ex. 33b as six-*one*.

Ex. 33h. Repeat Ex. 33g, sounding the first bracketed tone in your mind with its number in the original key, but singing it with its number in the new key: hear mentally six, sing it as *one* in the new key. With practice you will learn to discover which link tones in a passage make the transfer to a new key most convenient.

Ex. 33i. Exs. 33b to 33f acquaint the student visually and aurally with modulations from C to its near-related keys. Melodies obviously start in other keys and modulate. The student should rewrite and practice Exs. 33b to 33f in as many keys as possible so as to become visually acquainted with modulations in other keys.

Students seeking an easier approach to modulatory melody occasionally sing all the tones by number (or syllable) as if no change of key occurs. This is possible when no foreign (chromatic) notes appear; the musical student, singing a cadence on 5, will feel that it is really 1 in the dominant key. When chromatic notes signifying a modulation appear in the melody, singing the notes by scale numbers in the original key not only feels false, but increases the difficulty of rendering the notes accurately.

Compound Meter: Half Subbeat Values

Any subbeat of the beat unit in compound meter may be divided in half. In the following exercises, look for the beginning of each main beat in the measure.

Ex. 34a.   Clap the rhythms in Fig. 75, then sing with *la*.

Fig. 75

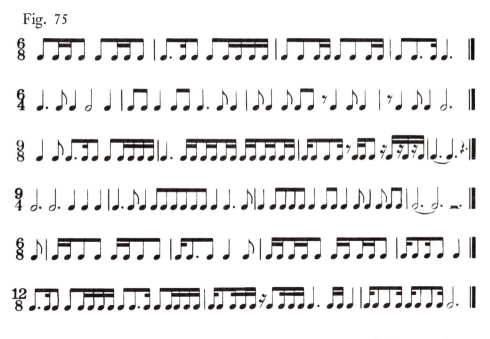

Ex. 34b.   Write two-measure units from each line of Fig. 75 from memory.

The Triplet in Simple Meter, Subdivided

Each third-of-a-beat value of a one-beat triplet may be divided in half. Compare the rhythms in Ex. 34c with those in Ex. 34a.

Ex. 34c.   Clap the rhythms in Fig. 76, then sing with *la*.

Fig. 76

Ex. 34d. Read the notes of the melodies of Section 6 by scale step numbers without singing them. Try to develop facility in reading them quickly.

Compound Meter: The Subbeat Divided in Half

5   Allegretto   Byrd

mp   *mf*

6   Scherzando   Vivaldi

rall. e dim.   *p*

mf

ritard.

7   Dolente   Spain

mp

p   *pp*   *rall.*

8   Allegretto   Mendelssohn

mp

VI   *mf*   *p*

9 ANIMATO LEGRENZI

10 MODERATO BYRD

11 GESANGVOLL GERMANY

12 MODÉRÉ LULLY

D. C. AL FINE

13   SPIRITED   ENGLAND

14   MARCATO   HANDEL

15   ANDANTE   BERLIOZ

16   ALLEGRO   BACH

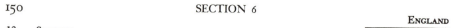

SECTION 6

151

17 Grazioso   Mozart

18 Andantino   England

19 Andante, doloroso   Rubinstein

20   LUSTIG   GERMANY

21   ALLEGRO, CON SPIRITO   BEETHOVEN

22   ANDANTE   BACH

23   LARGO   HANDEL

Simple Meter: The Third-of-a-beat Divided in Half

Modulation: Major to the Dominant Key

32 ALLEGRETTO, GRAZIOSO E LEGGIERO FEDELI

33 PLAYFULLY ENGLAND

34 LEGER FRANCE

FINE DAL SEG. AL FINE

35 MAESTOSO   METHFESSEL

36 PESANTE   GERMANY

37 ALLEGRO MOLTO   BEETHOVEN

38 GAILY   ENGLAND

42   GESCHWIND   GERMANY

43   BROADLY   ENGLAND

44   MODERATO   KLEIN

45   ANDANTINO   LECOCQ

46 ALLEGRETTO   HAYDN

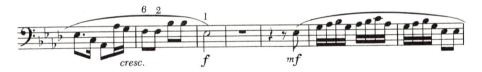

47 SEHNSUCHTVOLL   SILCHER

48 ANDANTINO   ENGLAND

49 ALLEGRO, MARZIALE   NÄGELI

50   LARGHETTO   FRANCE

51   ALLEGRO   CZECHOSLOVAKIA

52   LIEBLICH   SILCHER

53 **Allegretto**   **Schubert**

54   **Leggiero**   **Schumann**

55   **Vivace**   **Corelli**

59 SPIRITED WALES

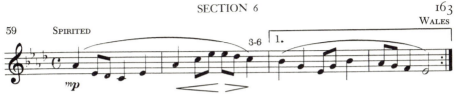

60 ANDANTE CON MOTO GREENE

61 FRÖHLICH AUSTRIA

FINE

DAL SEG.
AL FINE

62   ALLEGRETTO   LECOCQ

63   SCHERZANDO   OFFENBACH

64   POMPOSO   SACCHINI

65   ANDANTE   GRIEG

66   ANDANTINO   CORELLI

67   ANDANTE, CANTABILE   %   ROSSINI

DAL SEG.
AL FINE

Modulation: Major to the Relative Minor Key

72   **GESANGVOLL**   **GERMANY**

73   **ALLEGRO**   **NORWAY**

74   **ALLEGRO, RISOLUTO**   **RIGHINI**

75   **LIGHTLY**   **RUSSIA**

76 Vigorously   England

mf

mp   *cresc.*   *mf* *f*

77   Andante, cantabile   Brooman

p

Fine *mp*

p   dal Seg.
al Fine
Berlioz

78 Gracieux

p

mf *mf*

79 Cheerily

f   *rit.*   *pp* *cresc.*

Mac dowell

ff   *dim.*   Fine

Modulation: Major to the Relative Minor of the Dominant Key

83 FRÖHLICH ZUMSTEEG.

84 GAI OFFENBACH

85 LARGHETTO, NON TANTO BELLINI

*Notes marked (♯) may be sung without the accidental.

92 Langsam   3   6   1   3   Schumann

93 Decidé   Meyerbeer

mf

94 Andante, appassionato   Verdi

95 Andante   Smetana

96   LEGER   LECOCQ

Modulation: Major to the Subdominant Key

97   MODERATELY FAST   ENGLAND

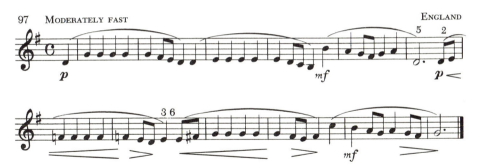

98 ALLEGRO, NON TROPPO   BACH

99 ALLEGRETTO   HAYDN

100 LARGE   LULLY

101 ANDANTE, CON MOTO   SCHUMANN

106   ANIMATO   MASCAGNI

107   ALLEGRO   ENGLAND

108   EINFACH   SCHUMANN

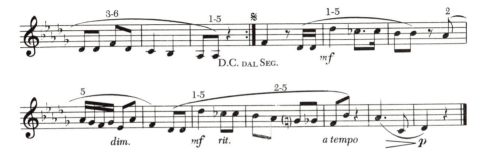

Modulation: Major to the Relative Minor of the Subdominant Key

112   **ALLEGRETTO**   **PAESIELLO**

113   **AUSDRUCK VOLL**

                                       MÜLLER-HARTUNG

114   **ENERGETICALLY**   **WALES**

115 GRACEFULLY   PURCELL

mf   *p*

mf   *mp*

mf   *p*

116 ANDANTINO   LISZT

cresc.   *mf*   *p*   *semplice*

un   poco accel.

e   cresc.   *mf*

un poco   rit.   *dim.*   *p*

117 ADAGIO, MA NON TROPPO   BEETHOVEN

p cantabile

sf

sf   *f > p*

118   MODERATO   BACH

119   LANGSAM   WENNERBERG

CHAPTER
9

Near-related Modulations from Minor Keys

THERE are five near-related keys to which a melody in minor may modulate. These are: 1) its relative major; 2) the dominant minor; 3) the relative major of the dominant minor; 4) the subdominant minor; 5) the relative major of the subdominant minor. Thus the near-related keys of a minor are C, e, G, d, and F.

Ex. 35a. Minor to relative major: Write out the following tones; sing them first by number, then with *la*. (a-C) 1-3-5-4-3-2-1-3, 1-3-5-4-3-2-1; 1-2-3-2-1, 6-5-8-2-7-8; 1-2-7-1-2, $\bar{7}$ 1-$\bar{6}$-$\bar{7}$-1; 1-2-3-4-4, 2-3-4-5-1; 5-3-1-6-5-5, 3-1-$\bar{5}$-4-3; 1-5-1-6-6, 4-2-4-$\bar{7}$-1.

Ex. 35b. Minor to dominant minor: Write the tones and sing as in Ex. 35a: (a-e) 1-2-$\bar{7}$-1-5-1, 4-5-2-3-2-1; 1-$\bar{5}$-1-2-2, 5-6-4-3-1; 1-$\bar{7}$-1-2-3, 6-6-5-4-3-2-1; 1-2-$\bar{7}$-1-5, 1-2-$\bar{7}$-1.

Ex. 35c. Minor to relative major of dominant minor: Write the tones and sing as in Ex. 35a: (a-G) 1-$\bar{5}$-$\bar{6}$-$\bar{7}$-1-1, 2-$\bar{7}$-1-2-3; 3-2-4-3-5-2, 3-2-4-3-5; 1-3-5-1-4-4, 5-4-3-2-3; 3-2-3-4-$\bar{5}$-5, 6-5-6-7-8; 3-5-$\bar{6}$-7-8-5-6, 7-8-5-6-7-8.

Ex. 35d. Minor to subdominant: Write the tones and sing as in Ex. 35a: (a-d) 1-$\bar{7}$-1-1, 5-6-5-2-3-1; 5-1-$\bar{7}$-2, $\bar{6}$-2-$\bar{6}$-$\bar{7}$-1-$\bar{5}$; 1-$\bar{5}$-3-$\bar{7}$-1-2-3-4, 1-$\bar{5}$-3-$\bar{7}$-1; 1-3-4-5-5, 2-2-5-2-4-3; 8-5-6, 3-2-5-6-4-2-$\bar{7}$-1.

Ex. 35e. Minor to relative major of subdominant: Write out the tones and sing as in Ex. 35a: (a-F) 1-2-$\bar{7}$-1-3, 5-8-7-8; 1-2-$\bar{7}$-1-1, 3-4-2-3; 3-5-4, $\bar{6}$-1-$\bar{6}$-$\bar{7}$-1-$\bar{7}$-2-1; 8-7-6-5-5, 7-6-7-8-5; 5-1-5-6-6, 1-$\bar{5}$-2-3-1.

Ex. 35f. Apply the instructions of Exs. 33g, 33h, and 33i to Exs. 35a-35e.

Minor Seventh Chords

Minor seventh chords, sometimes called *small seventh* chords, are formed by adding a tone to the minor triad which is a minor seventh above the root of the triad. II, VI, and III in major become II⁷, VI⁷, and III⁷; the IV in minor becomes IV⁷.

Ex. 36a. Write the II⁷ chord (2-4-6-8) in all major keys in the following patterns: 2-4-6-8; 8-6-4-2,5; 2-6-4-8; 8-4-6-2,5; 4-6-8-2,2-8-6-4,5; 6-1-2-4,4-2-1-6,5; 1-2-4-6,6-4-2-1,7. Practice singing these tones.

Ex. 36b. Write the VI⁷ chord (6-1-3-5) in all major keys in the following patterns: 6-1-3-5,5-3-1-6,2; 1-3-5-6,6-5-3-1,4; 3-5-6-8,8-6-5-3,2; 5-6-8-3,3-8-6-5,2. Practice singing these tones.

Ex. 36c. Write the III⁷ chord (3-5-7-2) in all major keys in the following patterns: 3-5-7-2,2-7-5-3,6; 5-7-2-3,3-2-7-5,6; 7-2-3-5,5-3-2-7,1. Practice singing these tones.

Ex. 36d. Write the IV⁷ chord (4-6♭-8-3) in all minor keys in the following patterns: 4-6-8-3, 3-8-6-4,2; 6-1-3-4, 4-3-1-6,5; 1-3-4-6, 6-4-3-1, 2; 3-4-6-8, 8-6-4-3,2. Practice singing these tones.

The Tenor Clef

Music for the tenor voice is sometimes written on the treble staff with a double G clef, 𝄞𝄞 , indicating that the notes are to be read on this staff but sung an octave lower than written. When the C clef is placed on the fourth line of a staff, that staff becomes the *tenor* staff; the C clef is then called the *tenor clef*. Fig. 77 demonstrates the relationship of this staff to the lines and spaces of the treble and bass staves.

Fig. 77

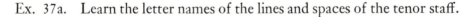

Ex. 37a. Learn the letter names of the lines and spaces of the tenor staff.

Ex. 37b. Read the notes of melodies on the tenor staff in Section 7 by letter name.

Tenor Clef Transposition

Melodies in the treble staff may be transposed from the original key to keys with the next lower letter by substituting the tenor clef for the G clef. Thus a melody in C or C♯ can be read in B or B♭. Proceed as follows. Copy the tenor clef signatures of Fig. 78. If, for example, a melody is in C or C♯, cover the original signature with the tenor clef signature of B or B♭. Read the notes in the tenor clef.

Fig. 78

Ex. 37c. Transpose melodies in the treble staff in Section 7 in the manner described, reading the notes by letter name in the tenor staff.

Melodies in the bass clef may be transposed by this method from the original key to keys a fourth lower or fifth higher: as C or C♯ to G or G♭.

Ex. 37d. Transpose melodies in the bass staff in Section 7, using the tenor staff. Cover the bass clef signature with a tenor clef signature of a key lettered a fourth below, and read the notes by letter name.

The Major Seventh

The interval of a *major seventh* is a semitone smaller than a perfect octave and encompasses seven letters—in C major, C-B. The scale steps 1-7 and 4-$\underline{3}$ in major, and 1-7, 3-$\underline{2}$, and $\overline{6}$-5 in minor (harmonic) are major sevenths.

Ex. 38a. Name by letter a major seventh up from each note in Fig. 23, then sing major sevenths up from each tone. First practice: 1-3-5-8-7, 1-8-7,1-7; sing the tones 1-7 with *la*.

Ex. 38b. Name by letter a major seventh down from each note in Fig. 23, then sing major sevenths down from each tone. Practice: 8-7-1, 7-1; sing the tones 7-1 with *la*.

Major Seventh Chords

Major seventh chords are formed by adding a tone which is a major seventh above the root of a major triad. In major the I⁷ (1-3-5-7) and the IV⁷ (4-6-8-$\underline{3}$) are major seventh chords; in minor the VI⁷ ($\overline{6}$♭-1-3-5) and III⁷ (3-5-7♭-$\underline{2}$) are major sevenths.

Ex. 38c. Write out the I⁷ and IV⁷ in every major key; the VI⁷ and III⁷ in every minor key.

Ex. 38d. Add the seventh scale step to Ex. 7e; practice singing the I⁷.

Ex. 38e. Practice the tones of the IV⁷, Ex. 36d, in major.

Ex. 38f. Practice the tones of the VI⁷ and III⁷ in minor following
  Exs. 36b and 36c.

The Half-diminished Seventh Chord

Review the diminished triad, Exs. 30c and 30e. The *half-diminished
seventh chord* is formed by adding a tone to a diminished triad which is
a minor seventh above the root of the triad. The II⁷ in minor (2-4-6♭-8)
and the VII⁷ in major (7̄-2-4-6) are examples of the half-diminished
seventh chord.

Ex. 39a. Write the II⁷ in minor for each key listed in Ex. 22b; write
  the VII⁷ chord in major for each key listed in Ex. 26a.

Ex. 39b. Practice singing the II⁷ in minor following Ex. 36a; practice
  singing the VII⁷ in major with these tones: 1, 7̄-2-4-6, 5; 1, 7̄-4-2-6, 5;
  5,6-4-2-7̄-1; 5, 6-2-4-7̄,1; 7̄-2-4-6,2-4-6-7, 4-6-7-2̲, 6̄-7̄-2̲-4, 3.

Ex. 39c. Read the notes of the melodies of Section 7 by scale step
  numbers without singing them. Try to develop facility in reading
  quickly.

Modulation: Minor to the Relative Major Key

4   **LANGSAM**   **FINLAND**

SCHNELLER

WIE ANFANGLICH

5   **GENTLY**   **ENGLAND**

6   **ALLEGRETTO**   **PERGOLESI**

7   **LANGSAM, FREI**   **HUNGARY**

8 LARGO, CON ABBANDONO   SPAIN

9 FROHLICH   GERMANY

10 ZIEMLICH SCHNELL   SWEDEN

11 SLOWLY   UNITED STATES

12   With vigor   England

13   Gracieux   France

14   Firmly   Wales

19 ANIMATED YOUNG

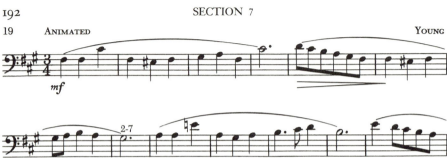

20 TRANQUILLY WALES

21 WUCHTIG SWEDEN

25 TEMPO GIUSTO BACH

26 DECIDE BIZET

27 GRAVE BOIELDIEU

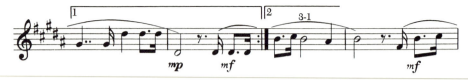

28 GRACEFULLY   4-2   ENGLAND

29 STARK   SCHUBERT

30 LARGHETTO   SPAIN

FINE

D.C.
AL FINE

31 TEMPO DI MINUETTO   PURCELL

32 WITH VIGOR   GREENE

FINE *mf*

D.C.
AL FINE

33   ALLEGRO   COUPERIN
                                                  2-7

mf

Modulation: Minor to the Dominant Minor Key

34   EXPRESSIF   FRANCE
                                                     2-5

p

1   5

mf

35   FAST AND LIGHTLY   ENGLAND

rit.   *p*

mp   *mf*   *cresc.*

3-5   1-3

f   [G]

36 CON FERVORE ROUMANIA

37 ALLEGRETTO MOZART

38 MODERATELY FAST ENGLAND

39   **Con moto**   **Brahms**

40   **Elegiaco**   **Gluck**

41   **Feurig**   **Kodaly**

42 Leggiero   Pergolesi

mf   *dim.*   Fine

mf

f   *f*   D.C.
                                                               AL FINE

43 Andante   Croatia

mf

f   *mf*

44 Playfully   United States

p

mf   *p*

45 Andante   Beethoven

mp   *dim.*   *p*   *p* *cresc.*

sf   *sf*

Modulation: Minor to the Subdominant Minor Key

49 SEHNSUCHTSVOLL   HUNGARY

50 MODÉRÉ   LULLY

51 ANDANTINO   HAYDN

52 ALLEGRO, NON TANTO   PERGOLESI

53 LARGO   RACHMANINOFF

SCARLATTI

Modulation: Minor to Related Major Keys other than the Relative Major

SMETANA

LORTZING

The Tenor Clef

61   BOLDLY   ENGLAND

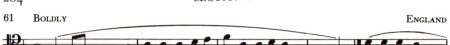

62   ANDANTINO   CALDERA

63   ALLEGRETTO   SWEDEN

64   ALLEGRO MARZIALE   DOHNANYI

65   GESANGVOLL   ARLBERG

66   ANDANTE SOSTENUTO   GLUCK

67   ALLEGRO, GIOCOSO   LOEWE

68   MACHTIG   GERMANY

(3)

69   LIEBLICH   REINECKE

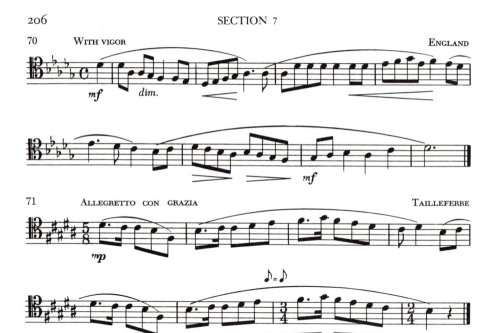

Minor

Seventh Chords

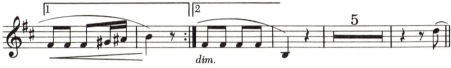

79   ANIMATED   ENGLAND

80   ANDANTE CON CALORE   GOUNOD

81   ADAGIO   VERDI

82   LEBHAFT   GERMANY

83   FRÖHLICH   POLAND

84   SEHNSUCHTVOLL   LINDBLAD

85   TRANQUILLO   SALIERI

86   ANDANTE   RUBINSTEIN

CHAPTER
10

Chromatic Tones

THE tones which lie within any major or minor scale are called diatonic tones. A melody in C which includes only C-major scale tones is a diatonic melody. Tones which are not diatonic tones may appear in a melody, and are called *chromatic tones*. The chromatic tones are starred in Fig. 79. A melody which has a preponderance of chromatic tones is called a *chromatic melody*.

Chromatic tones are classified according to the way they are used. They may serve: 1) as nonharmonic tones in the key; 2) as sharped and flatted tones of chords in the key; or 3) as tones which imply a shift to a new key.

Our present concern is with the first of these functions, that is, chromatic tones which are nonharmonic within the key. Chromatic tones which move from a chord tone by a semitone down or up and return to the same chord tone are called *chromatic neighboring* or *auxiliary tones*. Fig. 79a illustrates chromatic neighboring tones. When the auxiliary, after its return to the chord tone, is followed by the opposite auxiliary and then the original tone, the melodic unit is called a *turn*. The symbol ⌣ over a note stands for a rapid turn pivoting around that note; the symbol ⌒ means an inverted turn which takes the lower

Fig. 79

auxiliary first. A sharp below the turn symbol $\underset{\sharp}{\sim}$ signifies the use of a chromatic lower auxiliary in the turn; a sharp above the turn symbol $\overset{\sharp}{\sim}$ a chromatic upper auxiliary. Turns are illustrated in Fig. 79b.

Fig. 79c illustrates chromatic tones used in a *changing-tone figure*. The figure starts with a chord tone, moves to an auxiliary, skips to the opposite auxiliary, and returns to the original tone. A skip from a tone to an auxiliary tone (see Fig. 79d) makes this tone an *appoggiatura*. Originally the term *appoggiatura*, which means a "leaning tone," was applied to any nonharmonic tone, such as a passing tone, on the accent or accented part of the beat. In early music this was often written as ♩♩ , ♪♩ , or ♩♪. The second of these tones shares its time value equally with the first, its appoggiatura. The more precise definition given here is commonly accepted today. Fig. 79e illustrates the chromatic passing tone; compare this with the diatonic passing tones in Fig. 26.

Chromatic Auxiliary Tones

In the following exercises, write out the tones in C major; practice singing them, then write the tones in several other major keys. This will enable you to recognize chromatic tones in other keys. In singing chromatic tones by scale-step number it is simpler to sing "two" while thinking "two-sharp" than to sing the awkward "two-sharp." The same applies in singing scale steps by syllables. You may prefer a distinctive syllable for each diatonic and chromatic tone:

1	1♯	2	2♯	3	4	4♯	5	5♯	6	6♯	7	8
do	di	re	ri	mi	fa	fi	so	si	la	li	ti	do
(doh)	(dee)	(ray)	(ree)	(mee)	(fah)	(fee)	(soh)	(see)	(lah)	(lee)	(tee)	

8	7	7♭	6	6♭	5	5♭	4	3	3♭	2	2♭	1
do	ti	tay	la	lay	so	say	fa	mi	may	re	rah	do

In writing the following exercises, place the accidental sharp or flat *before* the note, not after. Do not write scale-step numbers under your notes.

Ex. 40a. I chord: 1-3-2♯-3; 1-5-4♯-5; 3-2♯-3-$\bar{5}$-5-4♯-5; 5-4♯-5-3-2♯-3-
1-$\bar{7}$-1. IV: 1-4-3-4-6-5♯-6-5; 8-7-8-6-5♯-6,5. V: $\bar{5}$-4♯-$\bar{5}$-$\bar{7}$-$\bar{6}$♯-$\bar{7}$-2-
1♯-2,3; 1,$\bar{7}$-$\bar{6}$♯-$\bar{7}$-5-4♯-5-2-1♯-2,3. V⁷: $\bar{5}$-4♯-$\bar{5}$-4,$\bar{7}$-$\bar{6}$♯-$\bar{7}$-4,2-1♯-2-4,3;
1,4-2-1♯-2,4-$\bar{7}$-$\bar{6}$♯-$\bar{7}$,4-$\bar{5}$-4♯-$\bar{5}$,1; $\bar{5}$-$\bar{7}$-$\bar{6}$♯-$\bar{7}$,5-2-1♯-2, $\bar{5}$-4-3-4,$\bar{5}$-5-4♯-5,1.

The student will find scale step 3♯ in some minor melodies as a lower auxiliary of scale step 4; this should not be mistaken for a modulation to the tonic major.

Chromatic Tones in the Turn and in Changing Tone Figures

Ex. 40b. I: 1-2-1-$\overline{7}$-1; 3-4-3-2♯-3; 5-6-5-4♯-5; 1-$\overline{7}$-1-2-1; 3-2♯-3-4-3; 5-4♯-5-6-5 (minor) 5-6♭-5-4♯-5; 5-4♯-5-6♭-5. IV: 1, 4-3-4-5-4; 6-5♯-6-7-6; 8-7-8-$\underline{2}$-8. V and V⁷: $\overline{5}$-6-$\overline{5}$-4♯-$\overline{5}$; $\overline{7}$-1-$\overline{7}$-$\overline{6}$♯-$\overline{7}$; 2-3-2-1♯-2,3; 4-5-4-3-4,3; $\overline{5}$-$\overline{4}$♯-$\overline{5}$-$\overline{6}$-$\overline{5}$; $\overline{7}$-$\overline{6}$♯-$\overline{7}$-1-$\overline{7}$, 2-1♯-2-3-2,1.

Ex. 40c. Write these tones in C, practice singing them, then write them in other major keys. I chord: 1-2-$\overline{7}$-1, 3-4-2♯-3, 5-6-4♯-5; 5-4♯-6-5, 3-2♯-4-3, 1-$\overline{7}$-2-1; 1, 3-2-4-3, 5-4♯-6♭-5; 5-6♭-4♯-5,3-4-2-3, 1; IV: 1-4-5-3-4, 6-7-5♯-6, 8-$\underline{2}$-7-8; 8-7-$\underline{2}$-8, 6-5♯-7-6, 4-3-5-4, 3. V and V⁷: $\overline{5}$-6-$\overline{4}$♯-$\overline{5}$, $\overline{7}$-1-$\overline{6}$♯-$\overline{7}$, 2-3-1♯-2,4-5-3-4, $\overline{5}$-$\overline{4}$♯-$\overline{6}$-$\overline{5}$, $\overline{7}$-$\overline{6}$♯-1-$\overline{7}$, 2-1♯-3-2, 1.

A series of melodic tones which includes a number of chromatic tones may look difficult and confusing to the student; with practice he will learn to see the passage as a single unit which may be nothing more than a simple I or V chord with chromatic auxiliaries, or changing or passing tones.

Mixed Half- and Third-of-a-beat Values in Simple Meter

In some melodies the beat unit is divided in half and in thirds. When both types of division do not fall in the same measure, practice the rhythm as in Ex. 41a.

Ex. 41a. Tap steady beats, for example, 2/4 1-2, 1-2; then clap evenly divided beats as follows: 2/4 1 2 | 1 2 | 1 2 | 1 2 :‖

As preparation for measures which contain both types of division, divide each beat in six, as in Ex. 41b. This exercise must be mastered before continuing.

Ex. 41b. Clap the following four measures, counting aloud with the counting given; then continue clapping, but count silently. Listen intently to the proportions of the values as you clap so that you can finally drop the fractional counting. Avoid ♪♫ or ♫♪ for the triplet.

2/4 1 2 3 4 5 6 1 2 3 4 5 6 | 1 2 3 4 5 6 1 2 3 4 5 6 | 1 2 3 4 5 6 1 2 3 4 5 6 |

Ex. 41c. First tap a steady two beats in 2/4, then clap evenly divided

(1)   (2)   (1)   (2)

beats as follows: 2/4   1   2   1 2 3 :‖ and   1 2 3   1   2 :‖

Ex. 41d. Clap the rhythms of Fig. 80, then sing with *la*.

Fig. 80

Ex. 41e. Write four-measure units from each line of Fig. 80 from memory.

The Duplet in Compound Meter

Just as the beat in simple meter was divided in half and in thirds in Ex. 41, so may the superbeat in compound meter be divided. The beat in compound meter is a composite of a main beat and two subbeats, a division in thirds. When the superbeat is divided in half, the rhythm

unit is a duplet: 6/8 ♩. = ♫; 6/4 ♩. = ♩♩ Compare Ex. 41b with Ex. 42a. The rhythms are similar and the approach to the rhythmic problem is the same; the only difference is that the beat unit in Ex. 42a is a dotted note.

Ex. 42a. Divide each beat in six and count as indicated; then follow the directions given in Ex. 41a.

Ex. 42b. Tap two superbeats to a measure, then divide each beat alternately in two and three.

Ex. 42c. Clap the rhythms in Fig. 81, then sing with *la.* Fig. 81 shows that the duplet value is written in different ways, sometimes in larger note-values: 6/8 ♫ ; less often as dotted notes, ♪♪. 6/4 ♩ ♩ ♩. ♩.

Fig. 81

Ex. 42d. Write four-measure units from each line of Fig. 81 from memory.

Chromatic Passing Tones, Between Chord Tones of I, IV, V, and V⁷

Ex. 43a. Write the following tones in C, practice singing them, then write them in other major keys. I: 1-2-2♯-3, 3-4-4♯-5, 5-6-6♯-7-8; 1-1♯-2-2♯-3; 5-5♯-6-6♯-7-8; 8-7-6-6♭-5; 8-7-7♭-6-6♭-5; 5-4♯-4-3, 3-2-2♭-1; 3-2♯-2-2♭-1. IV: 1-4-5-5♯-6,5; 1-4-4♯-5-5♯-6,5; 1-6-6♯-7-8; 1-2-2♯-3-4,3; 1-1♯-2-2♯-3-4,3; 8-7-7♭-6,5; 8-6-5-5♭-4,3; 3,5-6-4-3-2-2♭-1. V: 5̄-6̄-6♯-7̄-2,1; 7̄-1-1♯-2-5,3; 5-5♯-6-7,8; 5-5♯-6-6♯-7-8; 2-3-4-4♯-5-2,3; 2-2♯-3-4-4♯-5-7̄,1; 1-7̄-6̄-6♭-5̄,1; 3,2-2♭-1-7̄,1; 5-4♯-4-3-2,3. V⁷: 5̄-7̄-2-2♯-3-4; 5̄-6̄-6♯-7̄-2-4,3; 5̄-5♯-6̄-6♯-7̄-4,3; 5̄-7̄-1-1♯-2-4,3; 3, 4-3-2♯-2-7̄-5̄,1; 3,4-2-2♭-1-7̄-5̄,1; 3,4-2-7̄-6̄-6♭-5̄,1.

Scale step 3♯ in c minor may be used as a chromatic passing tone. This should not be mistaken for a shift to major.

Appoggiaturas with Chromatic Tones

Scale tones chromatically raised tend to resolve *up* by semitone. Such tones approached by a skip from above (appoggiatura) generally resolve up. Lowered scale tones tend to resolve *down* by semitone; used as appoggiaturas, they are generally approached by a skip from below. In singing these tones, think of the resolution tone as a temporary device; for example, in 5-2♯-3, think 5-3, then 5-2♯-3.

Ex. 43b. Write the following tones in C, practice singing them, then write the tones in several other major keys and sing the tones you have written. I: 1-5-2♯-3; 1-8-4♯-5; 8-2♯-3-1; 5-3-7̄-1; (minor) 1-3-6♭-5. IV: 8-5♯-6-4,3; 8-6-3-4,3; 5-6-4-7̄-1; 5-4-7̄-6(♭),5; 5̄-6-2-1-4,3. V and V⁷: 8-7-4♯-5-4-2,3; 5-6̄♯-7̄-2-4,3; 5-1♯-2-4-7̄,1; 5-4̄♯-5̄,5-6̄♯-7̄,5-1♯-2,5-5̄-6♭-5, 7̄-6♭-5,2-6♭-5-4,3.

Scale step 7♭ is often used as an appoggiatura or upper neighbor for scale step 6 in minor.

A skip to a chromatic tone may simply represent an appoggiatura: that is, in C the tones G-C♯-D may represent a skip in the V chord with an appoggiatura, C♯. The *same* tones in a melody in C may signify a modulation to d minor: 4-7̄-1. It is not always possible to determine by the melody alone which interpretation to put on these tones. Subsequent melody tones may help to clarify it.

Appoggiaturas Approached from Successive Scale Tones

Ex. 43c. Write out the following tones in C major; sing the tones you have written, then rewrite them in other major keys. 3-1♯-2, 4-1♯-2, 5-1♯-2, 6-1♯-2, 7-1♯-2, 8-1♯-2,3; 5-2♯-3,6-2♯-3, 7-2♯-3, 8-2♯-3-1; 8-4♯-5, 7-4♯-5, 6-4♯-5,3; 1-5̄♯-6̄, 2-5̄♯-6̄, 3-5̄♯-6̄, 4-5̄♯-6̄, 5-5̄♯-6̄-7̄-5̄,1; 6-6̄♯-7̄, 5-6̄♯-7̄, 4-6̄♯-7̄, 3-6̄♯-7̄, 2-6̄♯-7̄,1.

We said that raised scale-tone appoggiaturas are approached from above and lowered tones from below. The opposite occasionally occurs. The appoggiatura may at times appear like an unprepared changing-tone figure: 5-4-2♯-3, instead of 3-4-2♯-3.

Ex. 43d. Write out the following tones in C major. Practice singing them, then write the tones in several other keys, and sing from the notes you have written. 5̄-1♯-2, 6̄-1♯-2, 7̄-1♯-2,3; 5̄-2♯-3, 6̄-2♯-3, 7̄-2♯-3, 1-2♯-3,1; 1-2-4♯-5, 1-4♯-5, 7̄-4♯-5, 6̄-4♯-5, 5-4♯-5,1; 1-4-5̄♯-6̄, 3-5̄♯-6̄, 2-5̄♯-6̄, 1-5̄♯-6̄, 7̄-5̄♯-6̄, 6̄-5̄♯-6̄, 5̄-5̄♯-6̄,5-1; 5-6̄♯-7̄, 4-6̄♯-7̄, 3-6̄♯-7̄, 2-6̄♯-7̄,8. Follow the same procedure in minor: 7̄-6̄♭-5̄, 1-6̄♭-5̄, 2-6̄♭-5̄, 3-6̄♭-5̄, 4-6̄♭-5̄, 5-6̄♭-5̄,1.

Near-related Modulations From Major Keys, Continued

Review modulation exercises 33 and 35. In those exercises a scale tone in the original key was also a scale tone in the new key: for example, 1 in C was also 4 in G. A chromatic tone in the original key may also be a scale tone in the new key: that is, 1♯ in C is also 7 in d minor.

Ex. 44a. Write out the following tones using a *single* note for the bracketed scale numbers. Sing the tones, thinking the chromatic tone, but singing it with its scale number in the new key.

(C) 5-4-3-2-1♯ (d) $\overline{7}$-2-4-6-5-4-3 (C) 4-3-2-$\overline{7}$-$\overline{5}$-1; (C) 8-5-8-7-7♭ (d) 6-5-4-3-2-1 (C) 2-5-$\overline{7}$-1; (C) 1-3-4-5-5♯ (a) $\overline{7}$-$\overline{5}$-8-2-3-4 (C) 2-6-7-5-1; (C) 1-3-4-4♯ (G) $\overline{7}$-4-3-2-1 (C) 5-6-5-4-3-1; (C) 5-8-5-8-7-7♭ (F) 4-2-$\overline{7}$-$\overline{5}$-3 (C) 6-5-4-2-5-3-5-8; (C) 5-3-1-2-2♯ (e) $\overline{7}$-$\overline{5}$-5-4-3-2-1 (C) 3-4-3-2-6-5-4-3-5-1; (C) 5-3-1-2-3-4-4♯ (e) 2-$\overline{7}$-$\overline{5}$-5-4-3-1 (C) 3-4-2-$\overline{7}$-1.

Ex. 44b. Rewrite Ex. 44a, starting from other major keys; then practice singing the tones from the notes you have written.

Near-related Modulations from Minor Keys

The modulations in Ex. 45a start from the key of a minor and end on a chromatic tone which is a scale tone in the new key.

Ex. 45a. Write out the following tones, using a single note for the bracketed scale numbers. Sing these exercises, thinking the chromatic tone, but singing it with its scale number in the new key.

(a) 8-7-8-5-6-5-4-3-5-3♯ (d) $\overline{7}$-6-5-3-1 (a) 4-6-5-4-3-5-8-7-5-8; (a) 8-5-3-2-1-1-2♭-4-6-2♭ (d) $\overline{6}$-$\overline{5}$-1-3-2-1-$\overline{7}$-1-3 (a) 6-5-8-7-8; (a) 1-2-3-5-8-4♯ (e) $\overline{7}$-6-5-4-3-1-1 (a) 5-6-7-8-2-3-2-7-8; (a) 1-3-5-8-7♮-6♯ (e) 2-$\overline{5}$-$\overline{7}$-2-5-4-3-2-1 (a) $\overline{5}$-$\overline{7}$-2-4-3-2-1; (a) 1-2-3-2-$\overline{7}$-$\overline{5}$-$\overline{7}$-1-1♯ (F) 4-2-$\overline{7}$-$\overline{6}$-$\overline{5}$-$\overline{7}$-1-2-3 (a) 1-2-$\overline{7}$-1; (a) 1-3-5-6-6♯ (G)ˑ$\overline{7}$-2-5-4-3-5-8-8♯ (a) 7-2-5-4-3-5-8.

Ex. 45b. Rewrite Ex. 45a starting from other minor keys; then practice singing the tones from your written exercises.

Chromatic Auxiliary Tones

1   ZART   SCHUBERT

2   ALLEGRETTO   MEXICO

3   MODERATO   PORTER

4   ALLEGRO CON GRAZIA   VERDI

5 GEMACHLICH

MAHLER

mp   *cresc.*

mp

mf

6 ALLEGRO

PARTICHEKA

mf

7 GESANGVOLL

GERMANY

p

8 ALLEGRETTO

MOZART

mp

cresc.   *mf*

9 AIMABLE

OFFENBACH

p   *p*

10   ALLEGRETTO   ROSSINI

11   ANDANTE CON MOTO   BOIELDIEU

12   LEGGIERO   BEETHOVEN

13   FEURIG   HUNGARY

14   EINFACH   SCHUBERT

FINE

mf   DAL SEG.
                                           AL FINE

15   ANIMATO   VERDI

16   CARESSANT   BIZET

17   ENERGETICALLY   UNITED STATES

18   MODERATO   FIORAVANTE

19   VIVACE   DONIZETTI

Chromatic Auxiliary Tones in Minor and in Modulation

20   DOLENTE   ROSSINI

21 NICHT ZU LANGSAM BRAHMS

22 ANDANTE, SOSPIRANDO ITALY

23 SANFT SCHUBERT

24 LEISE   POLAND

25 MODERATO   SWEDEN

Chromatic Tones in the Turn

26 ALLEGRETTO   MOZART

27 VIVACE   CHOPIN

28 LEGER — GOUNOD

29 ANDANTE — SCARLATTI

30 LARGO — BEETHOVEN

31 MODERATELY FAST — ENGLAND

FINE

DAL SEG.
AL FINE

32   ALLEGRETTO GRAZIOSO   DVORAK

p *molto espressivo*

33   ANDANTINO   ROSSINI

Changing Tones

34   ALLEGRETTO   CHOPIN

35   DOULOUREUX   GRETRY

36   ALLEGRO CON BRIO   BEETHOVEN

37   DOLCE   NORWAY

38   FROHLICH   GOLDMARK

D.C.
AL SEG.

39   LARGO   BERLIOZ

40 ALLEGRO NON TANTO   VON WEBER

41 ALLEGRETTO   MOZART

Chromatic Passing Tones

42 DOLCE   SAINT-SAENS

43 ANDANTE   SCHUBERT

44 STARK   SCHUMANN

45 ALLEGRO NON TROPPO   HENSELT

46 MODERATO   RUBINSTEIN

47 SCHERZANDO   OFFENBACH

48 Larghetto   Lortzing

mp   *mf*

dim.   *mp*

49 Singend   Reichardt

mf   *dim.*

50 Moderato, con moto   Mozart

mf   *pp*

Fine *mp*   *p*   *cresc.*   D. C.

51 Breit   Germany

mf   *f*

mf

52 Largo   Adam

p

p

53   ALLEGRETTO   BERLIOZ

54   MÄSSIG, LIEBLICH   SCHUBERT

55   TEMPO COMMODO   VOLKMANN

56   DOLCE   DELIBES

57   ANDANTE CON MOTO, QUASI ALLEGRETTO   BERLIOZ

58   ALLEGRO   SCHUBERT

59   GAI   OFFENBACH

60 **ALLEGRETTO** **BEETHOVEN**

2-5   61   **LANGSAM, MIT GEFUHL**   **SCHUMANN**

62   **ALLEGRO**   **BEETHOVEN**

63 ANDANTE CANTABILE   BOITO

p

D.C.
DAL SEG.   *mf*

64   GAI   LECOCQ

dim.   rit.   **p**

mf   *dim.*   **p**

65 ALLEGRETTO   MESSAGER

p

66 ANDANTE   BEETHOVEN

p   3   3   3   3

mf   **p**

67 LENTO   MEYERBEER

p

5   4

mp   cresc.   (d♯ min.)   *mf*

3   4

p

68   AVEC FERVEUR   CHARPENTIER

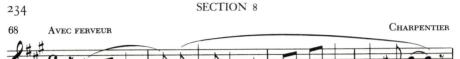

Chromatic Appoggiatura Tones

69   LENTO, CON MOLTO ESPRESSIONE   SCHUMANN

70   FEURIG   HUNGARY

D. C.
DAL SEG.

71   DOLCE, TRANQUILLO   FIELD

72 MODERATO   SACCHINI

mp

73 SCHERZOSO   SAINT-SAENS

p

74 SUAVE   LECOCQ

p   mf   p

mf   dim.   p

75 LUSTIG   LORTZING

mf

mp

76 ALLEGRO   THOMAS

mf (4#)

77 LEGGIERO   DIABELLI

f   mf   p

mf

dim.   p

78 ALLEGRO ADAM

79 ALLEGRETTO MOZART

80 LEISE BRAHMS

(c min.)

81 ANDANTE CON MOTO BALFE

82　ALLEGRO　　　　　　　　　　　　　　BEETHOVEN

mf

83　ANDANTE CON GRAZIA　　　　　　　FIORAVANTE

mp

mf　　　　　　　　　　　　　　　　　cresc.

mf　　　　　dim.　　　　　　　　　　p

84　LARGO　　　　　　　　　　　　　　HALEVY

mf　　　　　　　　　　　cresc.　　　f

mf

85　LANGSAM　　　BRAHMS

cresc.　　　　　　　　　　p

p　　　　　　　p　　　pp　ritard.

Simple Meter: the Beat Divided in Half and in Thirds

99   SUAVE   MEYERBEER

100   LENT   GOUNOD

101   ADAGIO   RACHMANINOFF

The Duplet in Compound Meter

102   MODERE   MASSENET

103   LEGER   LEROUX

104   BOLDLY   SULLIVAN

105   ANIMATO   MEXICO

106   MODERATO   VAUGHN WILLIAMS

107   AVEC CHALEUR   MESSAGER

108   ALLEGRO   GRIEG

109   INNIG   SCHUMANN

110   ANDANTE, MODERATO   VAUGHN WILLIAMS

111   GRAZIOSO   BRAHMS

112   ALLEGRO   MEXICO

113   GAI   FRANCE

[e min.]

CHAPTER
11

Transient Modulations

A MELODY starting in C and cadencing in G may pass through a minor en route. Such passing modulations are called *transient modulations*. In near-related modulations the transient key is usually close to both the original and the new key: for example, in modulating from C to G: C-a-G, C-e-G; from C to a: C-d-a, C-F-a, C-e-a; from C to d: C-a-d, C-F-d; from C to e: C-a-e, C-G-e; from C to F, C-d-F, C-a-F. Cadences on V of the new key are common. A melody may modulate to several near-related keys before ending in the original key.

Embellishing Dominants

Every triad in a key, except the VII and the II in minor, may be preceded by a dominant-sounding chord erected on the fifth of the triad. For instance, the II in C, D-F-A, may be preceded by A-C♯-E-G. Such dominants are called *embellishing (attendant* or *secondary) dominants.* The symbol VofII (or whatever the triad is) is used to indicate an embellishing dominant.* The effect of these two chords alone is generally too transitory to establish the feeling of a change of key. The two chords may be regarded as *momentary* or *transient* modulations, and in that case the portions of melody in which they occur will be sung with scale-step numbers of the momentary key. The basic difference between a modulation, transient or otherwise, and the embellishing dominant and triad, is that subdominant IV or related harmony—the II or II⁷—appears in a modulation. In the absence of accompanying harmony, however, it is often difficult to distinguish transient modulations from embellishing dominants and their triads, since embellishing dominants followed by their triads may come at any point in a melody.

Ex. 46a.   Write out the embellishing dominants and their triads in every major key, following the pattern given for the key of C in Fig. 82.

Ex. 46b.   Practice singing Fig. 82 and your written exercises.

---

* Embellishing dominants of the V chord might be more specifically written as VofV, V⁷ofV, VII⁷ofV, V⁹ofV, and V⁹♭ofV, and VII⁷♭ofV (see Chapter 12, p. 277). The symbol VofV is used to stand for any of these chords. The symbol X⁷ may also be used.

Fig. 82

V of V

Vof II

Vof VI

Vof IV

Vof III

The Dominant Ninth Chord, V^9

A dominant ninth chord is formed by adding a third above a dominant seventh chord. In C major, this is G-B-D-F-A; in c minor, G-B-D-F-A♭. The chord normally resolves directly to I; or indirectly: V^9-V^7-I.

Ex. 47a.   Considering each note in Fig. 23 as tonic, write the V^9 chord in each major key; write the V^9 of each minor key listed in Ex. 22b.

Ex. 47b.   Play the root of each dominant ninth you have written, then sing up and down the tones of each chord.

Major and Minor Ninths

The interval from root to the top tone of each chord in Ex. 47a is a ninth. In major it is a *major* ninth, an octave plus a major second; in minor it is a *minor* ninth, an octave plus a minor second.

Ex. 48a.   Name by letter a major ninth up from each note in Fig. 23, then sing major ninths up from each tone. Start practice by singing 5̄-5-6, 5̄-6.

Ex. 48b.   Name by letter a minor ninth up from each note in Fig. 23, then sing minor ninths up from each tone. Start practice by singing 5̄-5-6♭, 5̄-6♭.

Ex. 48c.   Name by letter a major ninth down from each note in Fig. 23, then sing major ninths down from each tone. Start practice by singing 5-6-5-5̄, 6-5̄.

Ex. 48d.   Name by letter a minor ninth down from each note in Fig. 23,

then sing minor ninths down from each tone. Start practice by singing
5-6♭, 5-$\bar{5}$, 6♭-$\bar{5}$.

The Diminished Seventh Chord

Play the V^9 in c minor: G-B-D-F-A♭. Now play the chord minus
the root: B-D-F-A♭. This chord, a *diminished seventh chord,* is composed of superimposed minor thirds. The interval from root to seventh,
B-A♭, a *diminished seventh,* encompasses seven letters, B-C-D-E♭-
F-G-A♭. The interval of a diminished seventh is enharmonic with the
major sixth. The difference between the diminished seventh chord and
the half-diminished seventh chord is that the former has a diminished
seventh from root to seventh, and the latter has a minor seventh.

On the piano there are but three diminished seventh chords:
(1) G♯-B-D-F; (2) A-C-E♭-G♭; (3) A♯-C♯-E-G. We merely repeat
one of these three when we start on a different tone: B-D-F-A♭[G♯] is
the first chord respelled. These three chords have a variety of enharmonic
respellings depending on their function in a key.

The chord B-D-F-A♭ is a V^9 without a root in c minor. The chord
in c minor is called V^9 *incomplete* or *VII*^{7}. When used in C major it is
a V^9 incomplete with a flat, or VII$^{7♭}$. The root in both cases is the
leading tone of the key. This chord, composed entirely of minor thirds,
sounds the same in any inversion. Each tone, then, may be the leading

Fig. 83

tone of a key, major or minor, which is a semitone higher, as in Fig. 83a. Used in this way these chords are dominant in function.

Ex. 49a. The first tone of the first diminished seventh chord is used as the leading tone of a and A in Fig. 83a. Practice singing these four measures, first with $\overline{7}$-2-4-6, 5-3-1, then with *la*.

Ex. 49b. The second, third, and fourth tones of the first diminished seventh chord are used as leading tones in Fig. 83b. Write these out as in Fig. 83a and practice as directed in Ex. 49a. The respelling is in accord with each new key.

Ex. 49c. The other two diminished chords and their resolutions are given in Fig. 83c and Fig. 83d. Write these out and practice as directed in Ex. 49a.

Mixed Third- and Quarter-of-a-beat Values in Simple Meter

Ex. 50a. Clap strict beats in 2/4; then clap these four measures repeatedly, making sure that the triplets and sixteenth-notes are absolutely even: 2/4 ♩ ♩ | 𝄽 𝄽 | ♩ ♩ | 𝄽 𝄽 :||

Ex. 50b. Clap the rhythms in Fig. 84.

Fig. 84

Ex. 50c. Write two-measure units from the last three lines of Fig. 84 from memory.

Ex. 50d. Write in ties in the first three lines of Fig. 84; clap, then sing with *la*.

Distant Modulations

Modulations to keys which differ in signature from the key of departure by two or more sharps or flats are called *distant modulations*. The keys of such modulations are more evident in harmonized melody than in unaccompanied melody, which may have only a few tones to indicate the modulation. The following exercises will give the student understanding and aural experience of distant modulations and chord progressions associated with them. For a fuller understanding of distant modulation via chromatic harmony, consult a standard harmony text. The text indicates the key changes in the melodies for sight singing.

The Opposite Mode Modulation

One type of distant modulation moves toward a near-related key, but substitutes the tonic of the opposite mode; for example, C-V^7 of a minor to the I of a minor becomes C-V^7 of a minor to the I of A major. Opposite mode modulations from C would therefore be to A, E, D, g, and f. The first three modulations are very useful because they lead directly back to near-related keys. For example, in C to A, A is V of d; in C to E, E is V of a; in C to D, D is V of G. By the same logic, a melody in C will modulate to B, which is V of e.

Ex. 51a.   Rewrite Exs. 33b, 33d, 33e, and 33f, changing the second key to the opposite mode. Most of the bracketed tones are common tones. In some instances they are not, and a chromatic shift is required. C to A: 1-5-3-1-3, etc. C is 1 in C, C♯ is 3 in A. Sing the tones you have written.

Starting from a minor, opposite mode modulations may go to D, E, c, g, and f. The first leads to a near-related key: a-D, which is V of G; the second returns to the original key: a-E, which is V of a. The shift from a to A, which is V of d, is a similar modulation.

In these modulations the tonic of the new key comes at the end of a phrase, changes its function to V, and leads into the tonic of the coming key. Although a-B, which is V of e, also functions in this way, it is not an opposite mode modulation. A melody may of course modulate to the opposite mode of the same key: C to c, or vice versa.

Ex. 51b.   Rewrite Exs. 35b and 35d, changing the second key to the opposite mode; sing the tones you have written.

Sequential Modulations

A phrase or period may be sequentially repeated in a different key. The same or substantially the same phrase may therefore be repeated sequentially in a series of opposite mode modulations: C-D-E.

The Quartolet in Compound Meter

The beat in compound meter normally divided in three may be divided in four; so that in 6/8 ♩. = ♫♫ | . This is called a *quartolet*, and is also written as ♫♫. In 9/4 ♩. = ♩♩♩♩, also written as ♫♫. Compare the rhythms in Ex. 52a with those in Ex. 50b. Except that the beat units are different, the relative values are the same.

Ex. 52a. Clap the rhythms in Fig. 85, then sing with *la*.

Fig. 85

Ex. 52b. Write four-measure units of each line of Fig. 85 from memory.

Ex. 52c. Write ties into Fig. 85; then clap and sing the rhythms.

SECTION 9

Transient Modulations to Near-related Keys

1 ALLA MARCIA

VOLKMANN

3   MODERE   RAMEAU

4   LUSTIG   GERMANY

5   MODERE   BIZET

6   ALLEGRO MODERATO   A. SCARLATTI

7   ANDANTE CON MOTO   ARNE

8   THREE-VOICE CANON   CHERUBINI

7♭ [a]

[G]

[D]

[a]   [D]

9   ANDANTE ESPRESSIVO   SULLIVAN

mp

7-3
[E]   3   2
                                                   [f♯ min.]

[E]   [D]

[E]   [A]

10   Vif   DUNI

[c min.]

[Eb]

[g min.]

[Eb]   [Ab]

[Eb]   [Bb]   [Eb]

D. C. dal Seg.
al Fine

11   ANDANTINO   DONIZETTI

Fine   p

[c# min.]   [E]

[B]   [E]

[c#]   [E]

Three-voice Canon

14   PESANTE   HELLER

15   LIGHTLY   HUMPHREY

16   ANDANTE   CARISSIMI

20   SOLONNEL   GLUCK

21   ALLEGRETTO   CHILCOT

22   LARGO   FRESCOBALDI

23 Leger　　　　　　　　　　　　　　　　　　　　Delibes

Canon

24　　　　　　　　　　　　　　　　　　　　　　　Telemann

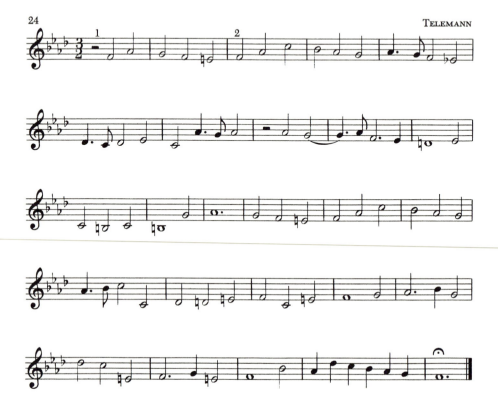

25 MIT HUMOR   MAHLER

26 VIGOROUSLY   IRELAND

27 LANGSAM   SCHUBERT

28 ALLEGRETTO   THOMAS

29 ZART   SCHUMANN

30   VIVACE   DITTERSDORF

31   MODERE   MASSE

32   FROHLICH   GERMANY

FINE

D. C. DAL SEG.
AL FINE

33   ALLEGRETTO   MEXICO

FINE

D.C. AL FINE

34   ESPRESSIVO   SALIERI

35   LANGSAM   SCHUBERT

36   ANDANTE CANTABILE   BELLINI

37   ALLEGRO NON TANTO   SPAIN

38   ANDANTE   MOZART

39   ALLEGRO   VILLA-LOBOS

The Quartolet

40   ADAGIETTO   RUBINSTEIN

[D]

mf

pp

41   ALLEGRO NON TROPPO   LISZT

mf   3   f

3

42   ANDANTE   FRANZ

p   cresc.

[F#]   dim.   p   [g# min.]

[B]

Embellishing Dominants

46 ANDANTE   MENDELSSOHN

47 LARGHETTO SOSTENUTO   FRANZ

48 FRÖHLICH   GERMANY

49   ALLEGRO VIVO   SCARLATTI

mp

3-6

VofIV

VofV   mf

50   ALLEGRETTO   CIMAROSA

p

VofII

51   MÄSSIG, GESCHWIND   SCHUBERT

f   mp

mf

VofVI   VofIV

52   ANDANTE, NON TROPPO LENTO   CACCINI

mf   piu f   p

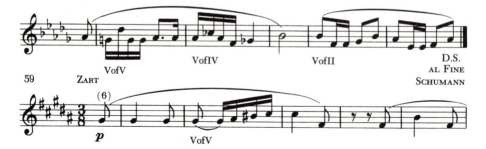

Embellishing Dominants Minor

Diminished Seventh Chords

Distant Modulation

71 ALLEGRETTO, GRAZIOSO — BRAHMS

72 ALLEGRETTO — SULLIVAN

73 ANDANTE — RACHMANINOFF

74 POCO LENTO E DOLCE — GRIEG

un poco piu animato

[F#] f# min.

espress.   rit.   F# maj.

75   ALLEGRO, COMMODO   DE FALLA

f con brio   3

3-1   3
3   [d] D

3   3

76   ANDANTE   (3♭)   PROKOFIEFF

mp   [C] c min.

5   1   >   1-5   > >
mf cantabile   *mf*   >

77   ANDANTE CON MOTO   SCHUBERT

p   *p*

6   4
G   [e min.] E

78   Moderato   SODERBERG

cresc.

Seq. mod.   mf

79   Allegretto   BRAHMS
(6)

dim.   p   p

Seq. mod.

Seq. mod.   G♯   rit.

80   Mässig   SCHUBERT

p   Seq. mod.

[e min.] E

CHAPTER TWELVE

CHAPTER
12

The Diminished Seventh Chord, Continued

COMPARE the general similarity of the following chords in C major: G-B-D-F, the V⁷; B-D-F, the VII; G-B-D-F-A, the V⁹; B-D-F-A, the VII⁷; G-B-D-F-A♭, the V⁹♭, and B-D-F-A♭, the V⁹♭ incomplete or VII⁷♭. They are all dominant in function and tend to resolve directly or indirectly to I. The last chord is a diminished seventh chord which can replace the V⁷ resolving to I. Similarly, the diminished seventh chord can replace the VofV, the VofII, and so on. The symbol *d*⁷ is used here to represent an embellishing diminished seventh chord.

Ex. 53a.   Practice singing Fig. 86.

Fig. 86

Ex. 53b.   Write out the embellishing diminished seventh chords and their triads in every major key, following the pattern for the key of C given in Fig. 86. Sing your written exercises with scale-step numbers and with *la*.

The Beat Unit Subdivided in Eight in Simple Meter

The beat unit in /2: 𝅗𝅥 subdivided in eight equals

The beat unit in /4: ♩ subdivided in eight equals

The beat unit in /8: ♪ subdivided in eight equals

Ex. 54a. Clap the rhythms in Fig. 87, then sing with *la*.

Fig. 87

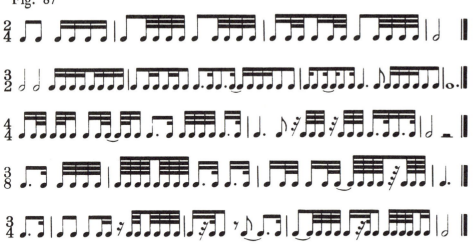

Ex. 54b. Write two-measure units of Fig. 87 from memory.

Ex. 54c. Write ties in each line of Fig. 87, then clap and sing the rhythms.

The Beat Unit Subdivided in Eight With Double Dotted Note

In this subdivision of the beat, the *second* of the two dots is equal to an eighth of a beat: 2/2 ♩..; 2/4 ♪..

Ex. 54d. Clap the rhythms in Fig. 88, then sing with *la*.

Fig. 88

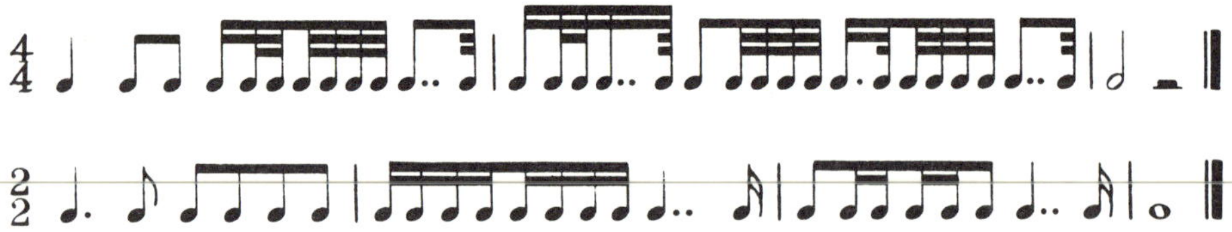

The Diminished Seventh Chord in Distant Modulations

Since any tone of a d⁷ chord may be a leading tone, all tones, except for the root, may be leading tones of distant keys; see Fig. 89.

Ex. 55. Practice singing Fig. 89. Starting from the other major keys, use the three diminished seventh chords in distant modulations.

Fig. 89

Fig. 90

The Supertriplet

The *supertriplet* is a triplet which extends duple and triple meter, and over two or four meter. Exercise 56 is confined to the use o triplet in simple duple meter and the half-mea quadruple meter. Practice 2/4 ♩ ♩ | ♩ ♩ ♩ a of 2/2 ♩ ♩ | ♩ ♩ ♩ ; practice 2/2 ♩ ♩ | ♩ ♩ ♩ a of 2/1 ♩ ♩ ♩ ♩ ♩ .

Ex. 56. Clap the rhythms in Fig. 90, then si

SECTION 10

Simple Meter: the Beat Divided in Eighths

281

5   ALLA POLACCA   BEETHOVEN

6   ANDANTE   MOZART

7   ALLEGRETTO   MEYERBEER

8   ANDANTINO   ROSSINI

9   ADAGIO, MOLTO ESPRESSIVO   BEETHOVEN

p   mezzo voce

10   LARGO   BACH

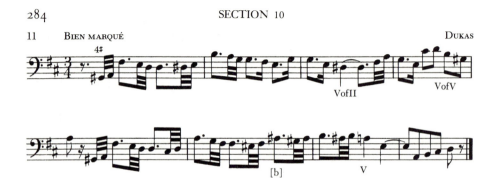

The Supertriplet

16 ALLEGRO   UNITED STATES

mf

FINE

17   ANDANTE CON MOTO   BORODIN

D.S.
al FINE   mp   f

18 GRANDIOSO   REGER

mf

19 ALLEGRETTO   SULLIVAN

mp

Diminished Seventh Chords

23   MAESTOSO   HAYDN

24   ANDANTE, NON TROPPO, LENTE   BERLIOZ

25   ANDANTE   BACH

26   ANDANTE   BRAHMS

13

The Supertriplet, Continued

THE rhythm in Fig. 91 consists of a combination of beats divided in half and the supertriplet in simple duple and quadruple meter. Practice 2/4 ♫ ♫ | ♩♩♩ as if it were one measure of 2/2 ♫♫ ♩♩♩; practice 2/2 ♩ ♩♩♩ | ♩ ♩ ♩ as if it were one measure of 2/1 (whole note): 2/1 ♩ ♩ ♩ ♩ ♩♩♩.

Ex. 57.   Clap the rhythms in Fig. 91, then sing with *la*.

Fig. 91

In simple triple meter the supertriplet occupies two of the three beats. As preliminary practice, count as follows: 3/4 123 456 789 | 12 34 56 789 :|| until you get the feel of relative durations.

The supertriplet in simple triple meter is combined at times with half-beat values. Practice this as follows: 3/4 12 34 56 78 and 9 | also 12 and 3 45 67 89 |. Make sure that beats 8-and, 2-and, get no more than a single beat.

Ex. 58.   Clap the rhythms in Fig. 92, then sing with *la*.

Fig. 92

Distant Modulations, Continued

Distant modulations may appear abruptly: for instance, from I of C to I of B. More often the keys are linked by a tone or chord which is common to both keys. In Fig. 93, notice that the tone F links the keys of a minor and Bb major; that the I of Bb becomes the VI of Db (F remaining as a common tone); and that the V of VI (Db) enharmonically becomes a chromatic chord in a, the IV⁷#.

Fig. 93

Schubert

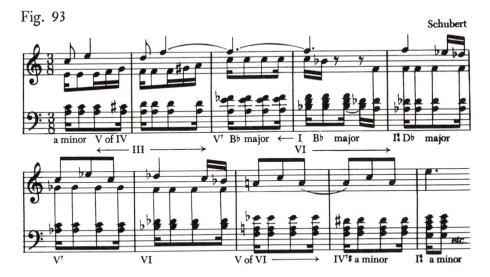

Common chords of distant modulations may be diatonic in both keys; diatonic in one key and chromatic in the other; or chromatic in both keys. Chromatic chords are a separate area of study, and should be studied before analyzing modulations of the second and third types.

Common Tones in Distant Modulations

Common chord modulations are infrequently evident in the melody alone. The following exercises are therefore confined to common tones between distant keys. These tones are shown in Figs. 94–96 with large noteheads.

Common tones in tonic chords of distant keys: A section of melody may close on I of the original key; the following section may begin on the same tone, or another tone of the I chord of the distant key; see Fig. 94a. Or the dominant may precede the tonic of the new key, Fig. 94b; additional chords in the new key are generally used to confirm that key.

Fig. 94

Ex. 59. Practice singing the key changes in Fig. 94a and b with scale-step numbers as shown in measure 1; then sing with *la*.

Common tones in dominant chords: A section of melody may move from a key to a distant key via a tone common to the V⁷ of each key; this is illustrated in Fig. 95. The second of these dominants may go to the tonic minor of the new key as well.

Fig. 95

Ex. 60. Practice singing Fig. 95 with scale-step numbers, then with *la*. Using G, B, and D, the other tones of the V⁷ in C, as common tones of V⁷s of distant keys, work out similar exercises and practice them.

Common tones in tonic to dominant: A tone in I of the old key is a tone in V⁷ of the new key, as is shown in Fig. 96.

Fig. 96

Ex. 61. Practice singing Fig. 96 with scale-step numbers, then with *la*. Using the other I chord tones in C—E and G—as tones common to dominants in distant keys, work out similar exercises and practice singing them. Do this also with the tones of the IV chord.

Subtriplets in Simple Meter

Subtriplets are triplets on the half-beat or less. As preliminary practice, clap half-beats. First count "one-and," "two-and;" then clap three even claps on the "ands." Compare triplets on half-beats in 2/4 with triplets in 4/8, illustrated in Ex. 27a.

Ex. 62a. Clap the rhythms in Fig. 97, then sing with *la*.

Fig. 97

Consecutive triplets on half-beats, 2/4 ⌐3⌐ ⌐3⌐ , are sometimes written as a *sextolet:* 2/4 ⌐6⌐ . Sextolets may occupy a half-beat or less: 2/4 ⌐6⌐ .

Ex. 62b.   Write each line of Fig. 97 from memory.

Ex. 62c.   Write ties into Fig. 97. Clap the rhythms, then sing with *la*.

Triplets in Compound Meter

The *subbeat* in compound meter may be a triplet.

Ex. 63a.   Clap the rhythms in Fig. 98, then sing with *la*.

Fig. 98

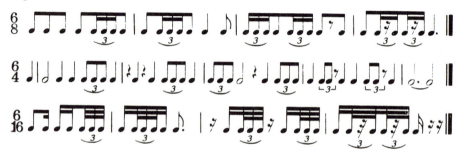

Ex. 63b.   Write two-measure units from each line of Fig. 98 from memory.

Ex. 63c.   Write ties into Fig. 98, then clap and sing with *la*.

Subtriplets in Simple Meter, Continued

Any or all the single values of a triplet in simple meter may be a subtriplet. Clap the first two measures of Fig. 99 repeatedly. Now clap a subtriplet on the last note of the triplet. Do the same with the first note; then with the second note. Compare the rhythms in Fig. 99 with those in Fig. 98.

Ex. 63d.   Clap the rhythms in Fig. 99, then sing with *la*.

Ex. 63e.   Write four-measure units of each line in Fig. 99 from memory.

Fig. 99

Ex. 63f.   Write ties into Fig. 99, then clap the rhythms and sing with *la*.

SECTION 11

Simple Meter: Triplets on the Half-beat

10 ADAGIO, MA NON TROPPO   BEETHOVEN

Compound Meter: Triplets on the Subbeat

11 POCO SOSTENUTO   DVORAK

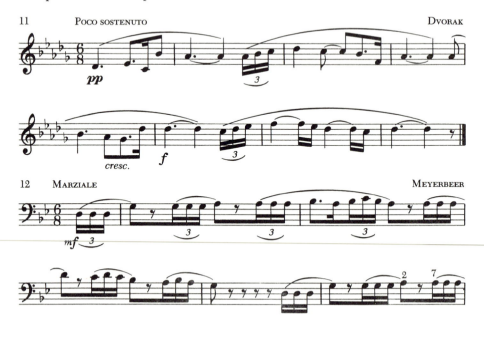

12 MARZIALE   MEYERBEER

13 ALLEGRETTO   GRIEG

14 MODÉRÉ   DAQUIN

15 LENTO CON MOTO   LOEWE

16 DOUX ET LEGER   MEYERBEER

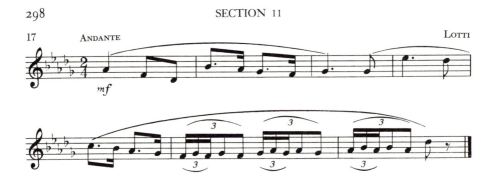

17   ANDANTE   LOTTI

Modulations via Common Tones

18   ALLEGRO   CZECHOSLOVAKIA

19   ANDANTE   LISZT

FINE

20   ALLEGRO   ALBENIZ

D. C. AL FINE

21 ANDANTE, ESPRESSIVO BRAHMS

VofIV

22 ANDANTE   GRIEG

mf

pp

23 MARZIALE   MAHLER

p   *mf*

ff

24 LARGHETTO   SCHUMANN

p

ab = g#   *mp*

29   ALLEGRETTO, GRAZIOSO   HUMPERDINCK

c♯ = D♭

30   GRANDIOSO   CHABRIER

3-1   5 =

d♯ = e♭

31   ANDANTINO   TSCHEREPNINE

3-4

3-5

CHAPTER
14

The Augmented Fifth and Sixth

WE have encountered the augmented second in the harmonic minor scale, 6-7; and the augmented fourth, 4-7, in major and minor. Any perfect or major interval which is enlarged by a semitone but which retains the same letters is called *augmented*. For instance, $\overline{\text{G-D}}$ is a perfect fifth; $\overline{\text{G-D}\sharp}$ and $\overline{\text{G}\flat\text{-D}}$ are augmented fifths. $\overline{\text{A-F}\sharp}$ is a major sixth; $\overline{\text{A}\flat\text{-F}\sharp}$ is an augmented sixth. These augmented intervals are characteristic of a number of chromatic chords and are occasionally found in melody.

Enharmonic Intervals

The music of nineteenth-century composers is replete with chromatic harmony involving chords like the diminished seventh and augmented fifth and sixth chords. Such chords are used both as chromatic chords in the key and as *pivotal* chords in a modulation. When diminished or augmented intervals of these chords appear in melody, spelled to conform to the spelling of the chord, we should nevertheless recognize the interval and translate it to an equivalent simpler form learned from interval-singing practice. For instance, we know the minor seventh; if an augmented sixth, which is its equivalent, occurs in the melody, we can recognize it and sing the interval with ease.

It is characteristic of contemporary music that tonal centers are either vague or nonexistent. Melody skips in tones unassociated with a tonal center are written now and then in strange-looking intervals. The student should therefore acquire facility in translating such enharmonic intervals into their simpler equivalents, which are listed below:

> augmented prime* (C-C♯) equals a minor second
> augmented second (C-D♯) equals a minor third
> augmented third (C-E♯) equals a perfect fourth
> augmented fourth (C-F♯) equals a diminished fifth
> augmented fifth (C-G♯) equals a minor sixth
> augmented sixth (C-A♯) equals a minor seventh
> augmented seventh (C-B♯) equals a perfect octave
> diminished second (C-D♭♭) equals a perfect prime

---

* The *perfect prime* consists of two tones on the same pitch; as such, it is not, by definition, an interval. When the tones are altered, C-C♯, an actual interval exists.

diminished third (C-Ebb) equals a major second
diminished fourth (C-Fb) equals a major third
diminished fifth (C-Gb) equals an augmented fourth
diminished sixth (C-Abb) equals a perfect fifth
diminished seventh (C-Bbb) equals a major sixth
diminished octave (C-Cb) equals a major seventh

Ex. 64a. Write all the augmented and diminished intervals up from each of the following notes: C#, Ab, B.

Ex. 64b. Write all the augmented and diminished intervals down from each of the following notes: Eb, F#, A.

The Beat Unit in Simple Meter, Subdivided in Sixteen

The rhythms in Fig. 101 may look formidable because of the large number of notes in a measure and the black look of the page. The rhythms become relatively easy, however, when each unit of four tones is treated as a single beat:

Fig. 100

Think, also, of 2/4 as 8/16; 3/4 as 12/16; and 4/4 as 16/16.

Ex. 65. Clap and sing the rhythms in Fig. 101.

Fig. 101

Modal Melody

Early Christian music, called *Gregorian chant*, is based on eight tonal systems or modes, four of which were called *authentic modes*. Gregorian modes governed the tonal character of religious and most secular music in Europe for over a thousand years. The ranges and *finals* or *concluding tones* (large noteheads) of the authentic modes are given in Fig. 102. A fifth mode, the Aeolian, was described above in Chapter Six. Each authentic mode has a tone of secondary importance, its *dominant*, designated in Fig. 102 by a whole note. Note that the range includes a tone below the final.

Fig. 102

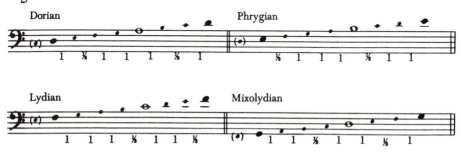

Except for a difference in tuning which is explained below, these modes correspond to the white key scales from d below middle C to the D above —the Dorian mode; the e below middle C to the E above—the Phrygian mode; f to F—the Lydian mode; and g to G—the Mixolydian mode. The note B♭ was frequently substituted for B to avoid the tritone F-B, a highly discordant interval because of the tuning system then in use. This alteration converts the Dorian to the Aeolian mode, and the Lydian to major.

Modal pitches before Bach's time were tuned by exact fifths, called *pure-tone tuning*. The exact fifth has a ratio of 2:3; for example, $\overset{2\ :\ 3}{C \rightarrow G}$. This yardstick was applied to successive fifths upward: $\overset{2\ :\ 3}{G \rightarrow D}$, $\overset{2\ :\ 3}{D \rightarrow E}$, and to fifths downward: $\overset{2\ :\ 3}{B♭ \leftarrow F}$, $\overset{2\ :\ 3}{F \leftarrow C}$ and so on.

Exact-fifth tuning resulted in two different pitches for tones which now have one pitch and one key on the keyboard; for example F♯ and G♭, C♯ and D♭. Fig. 103 illustrates the discrepancies which arose.

This tuning was clearly impractical for keyboard instruments, and created difficulties in vocal music as well. Melodies in the modes for keyboard instruments were largely confined to white-key notes. Singers

Fig. 103

$$G\flat \xleftarrow{\substack{2 \,:\, 3}} D\flat \xleftarrow{\substack{2 \,:\, 3}} A\flat \xleftarrow{\substack{2 \,:\, 3}} E\flat \xleftarrow{\substack{2 \,:\, 3}} B\flat \xleftarrow{\substack{2 \,:\, 3}} F \leftarrow C$$

$$C \xrightarrow{\substack{2 \,:\, 3}} G \xrightarrow{\substack{2 \,:\, 3}} D \xrightarrow{\substack{2 \,:\, 3}} A \xrightarrow{\substack{2 \,:\, 3}} E \xrightarrow{\substack{2 \,:\, 3}} B \xrightarrow{\substack{2 \,:\, 3}} F\sharp \rightarrow C\sharp \rightarrow G\sharp \rightarrow D\sharp, \text{ etc.}$$

did not have this problem. They could start a modal melody on any tone convenient for their vocal range.

The introduction of the major and minor modes, their harmonic requirements, and the need for modulation compelled a change in the system of tuning to the *tempered scale*, a compromise which made half-step intervals approximately equal and provided one pitch for both F♯ and G♭, C♯ and D♭. Tempered tuning also permitted the transposition of any white-key mode to any location on the keyboard. A melody in a transposed mode required the use of accidentals to preserve the modal pattern of whole and half steps, which raised a problem of a key signature. The original white-key modes required no signature.

Modal Signatures

Since the Lydian and the Mixolydian modes have a partly major quality, a major signature is utilized for these transposed modes. Thus the Lydian mode with G as final has these tones: G-A-B-C♯-D-E-F♯-G. In some melodies the borrowed signature is D (two sharps). The final looks curious, because we are accustomed to associating two sharps with a final tonic on D. More commonly a signature of one sharp is used, and the C sharps are written into the melody.

The Dorian and Phrygian modes lean toward minor, and therefore minor signatures were borrowed for these transposed modes: the Phrygian with D as final has these tones: D-E♭-F-G-A-B♭-C-D. The signature of g minor is used, or that of d minor with every E♭ written in. A melody in the Dorian mode with F as final has these tones: F-G-A♭-B♭-C-D-E♭-F. The signature may be either three flats, or four flats with each D♭ canceled.

Ex. 66a. Write out the Lydian mode, using the following notes as finals: A, B, D, E♭. Write out the Mixolydian mode with these finals: E, B♭, C♯, A♭.

Ex. 66b. Write out the Dorian mode with these finals: C, E, A, F♯. Write out the Phrygian mode with these finals: B, C♯, G, F.

The following exercises use chromatic scale steps in major, and afford practice in the Lydian and Mixolydian modes.

Ex. 66c. Write out the following major-scale tones, then sing with *la:* 1-2-3-4♯-5-2-4♯-3-1. Write out, then sing with *la:* 5̄-1-1-2-7̄♭-1-3-5-8-7♭-8-5-6-7♭-4-5.

Ex. 66d in minor affords practice in the Dorian and Phrygian scales.

Ex. 66d. Use the natural minor with the indicated chromatic changes, first writing the tones, then singing with *la:* 1-3-4-5-6♯-7-6♯-7-5, 2̲-7-5-8-6♯-4-6♯-5. Write out, then sing with *la:* 1-2♭-3-4-2-1, 5-6-5-4-1-7̄-2♭-1.

The modes were gradually supplanted by the major and minor scales, which offered a strong tonal center, harmonic skips in melody, and variety in key relationships. Modern composers, feeling that the resources of tonal melody and harmony have been well-nigh exhausted, have turned to the modes and to newly-contrived scales as additional sources for musical creativity.

Reading Melodies in the Modes

(1) Examine the key signature and look for accidentals in the melody. Is the melody in one of the major-like modes? Check the final and look for either the raised fourth step of the Lydian or the lowered seventh step of the Mixolydian. (2) Is the melody in one of the minor-like modes? Check the signature and the final. Look for the raised sixth step of the Dorian or the lowered second step of the Phrygian. The last note of a melody in one of the modes is not necessarily the final; ballads with a number of refrains often end on a tone other than the final which facilitates the return to the beginning.

The introduction of major and minor affected the modal character of composed vocal music and folksong. Consequently, a Dorian melody may have melodic fragments in the melodic (raised sixth and seventh) minor; it may have a contrasting middle section in the relative major. A Mixolydian melody may also include the raised seventh step of the major. Other hybrids include melodies in more than one mode. Check the melodies in Section 12 for these variants. Melodies with but five different tones (called *pentatonic* melody) or six different tones (*hexatonic*) are not uncommon in folk music.

Subtriplets in Compound Meter

Triplets on the *half-beat* in 6/8, 6/4, 9/8, 9/4, 12/8 and 12/4:

Ex. 67a. Clap the rhythms in Fig. 104, then sing with *la*. Make sure that you know where each superbeat begins.

Fig. 104

Ex. 67b. Write two-measure units from each line of Fig. 104 from memory.

Subtriplets on the Quarter-beat in Simple Meter

Ex. 68a. Clap the rhythms in Fig. 105, then sing with *la*.

Fig. 105

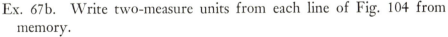

Ex. 68b. Write two-measure units from each line of Fig. 105 from memory.

The Subbeat in Compound Meter, Divided in Four

Four notes may occupy the time of any subbeat in compound meter. In Fig. 106, count each subbeat—for example, 1-2-3-4-5-6—clapping four times for the split subbeat.

Ex. 69a. Clap the rhythms of Fig. 106, then sing with *la*.

Fig. 106

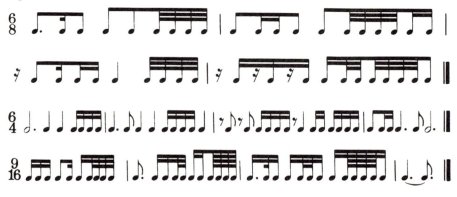

Ex. 69b. Write two-measure units of each line of Fig. 106 from memory.

Ex. 69c. Write ties into Fig. 106, then clap and sing the rhythms.

The Third-of-a-beat in Simple Meter, Divided in Four

Four notes may occupy the time value of any triplet note in simple meter. Compare the rhythms in Fig. 107 with those of Fig. 106.

Ex. 70a. Clap the rhythms in Fig. 107, then sing with *la*.

Fig. 107

Ex. 70b. Write two-measure units from each line of Fig. 107 from memory.

Ex. 70c. Write ties into Fig. 107, then clap and sing the rhythms with *la*.

Compound Meter, Continued

The subbeat in compound meter may be divided in two, three, or four.

Ex. 71. Clap the rhythms in Fig. 108, then sing with *la*.

Fig. 108

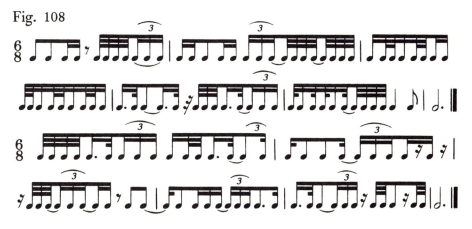

The One-beat Triplet and Supertriplet Combined

Review Exs. 27 and 57.

Ex. 72a. Clap rhythms of Fig. 109, then sing with *la*.

Fig. 109

Ex. 72b.   Write four-measure units from each line of Fig. 109 from memory.

Ex. 72c.   Write ties into Fig. 109, then clap and sing with *la*.

The Quintolet; Rhythm Groups Indivisible by Three or Four

Five tones, equal in duration, called a *quintolet*, may occupy one beat in simple meter: 2/4 ♩ ♫♫♩ ; occupy a superbeat in compound meter: 6/8 ♫♫♩ ♩ ♪; or two beats in simple meter: 4/4 ♫♫♩ ♩. ♪. The

Fig. 110

quintolet may occupy a fraction of a beat: 3/4 ♩. ♪♩♫♫♫ ; a sub-beat in compound meter: 6/8 ♩. ♩ ♫♫♫ ; or a fraction of a subbeat, 6/4 ♩. ♩ ♩ ♫♫♫ .

Any number of tones indivisible by three or four—seven, ten, eleven, thirteen, fourteen—may be used similarly. In doing Ex. 73 keep the tones of the quintolet and septolet even in duration. Do not distort the rhythm to ♫♫♫ ♫ or ♫♫♫ ♫♫♫ . Indivisible groups of ten or more tones are usually performed freely (*ad libitum*) by stretching out the beat.

Ex. 73. Clap the rhythms of Fig. 110, using a slow beat; then sing with *la*.

Rhythm and Meter in Contemporary Music

One definition of rhythm is that it is the relationship in duration between two or more tones. By that definition there is nothing new in the rhythms of modern music. The principal difference between modern and eighteenth- and nineteenth-century music is that rhythmic patterns used in the earlier period tend to be more regular and repetitious, while the rhythms used in contemporary music are subtler and more varied.

The subtlety of modern rhythm is achieved by a new treatment of accent and meter. Dynamic accents occur irregularly in the established measure, often implying a meter different from the metric signature; this is illustrated in Fig. 111a. These irregular dynamic accents are frequently acknowledged as metric accents, so that a scheme of constantly changing meters is set up; Fig. 111b shows how this is done. When there is a regular pattern of metric change, as in Fig. 111c, the composer indicates this by accents or a composite meter signature.

Unless otherwise indicated, a note value in one meter equals the same note value in a different meter: that is, a quarter note in 2/2 equals a quarter note in 3/4; a sixteenth note in 3/16 equals a sixteenth note in 2/8. Metric irregularity, producing half phrases and phrases of uneven length, gives greater plasticity to the melodic line.

Two different meters may occur simultaneously. This may be implied or overtly indicated. Regular offbeat dynamic accents in the melody line set up a meter which is different from that of the accompaniment, or a concurrent line in polyphony. *Polymeter*—two or more different and

concurrent meters—is often indicated by note beaming which crosses
bar lines (see Fig. 111d).

Fig. 111

Ex. 74.   Clap the rhythms of the melodies in Section 12, then sing them
with *la*.

Melody in Contemporary Music

The sense of a central tonality is either obscure or totally absent in
some contemporary melody. Major and minor scales and the harmony
derived from them have little or no relation to the melodic tone patterns
used in modern music. Instead, practically all contemporary melody
is based on contrived scales which generally span more tones than the
seven of the diatonic scales. Some tones in these contrived scales look
like chromatic tones in the major scale, such as 4♯, 7♭. They are, however, primary tones in a contrived scale; unrelated to a tonality, such
tones do not act as raised or lowered scale tones and therefore do not
necessarily resolve up or down by step.

One contrived scale treats all twelve tones within the octave as
equally important. The twelve tones occur in preset order, and every
tone must be used before the composer can return to any already used
in the melody. No single tone therefore emerges as a tonal center. This
approach is now generally modified in practice.

Key signatures for music without tonality are clearly useless. Modern
composers often use unorthodox signatures representing those sharped
or flatted tones which appear with greatest frequency in the melody.
Some use a simple orthodox signature and write in the sharps or flats
for additional tones in a contrived scale.

New chord concepts in modern harmony are reflected in the contour of contemporary melody. Chords built up in fourths like C-F-B(♭)-E(♭)-A(♭) provide the basis for melodic skips up or down in a series of fourths. Chords built up in thirds beyond the ninth—such as C-E-G-B-D-F-A, any tones of which may be altered—are reflected in melodic skips of sevenths, ninths, elevenths, and various augmented and diminished intervals. Chords consisting of bunched tones in seconds, tone clusters, and the combined tones of the whole-tone scale used as a chord, contribute novel and interesting melodic formations. Unlike the chords in eighteenth- and nineteenth-century music, these chords do not progress to a tonal center.

Up to this point, our sight singing has depended on gauging tones by their distance from the tonic tone. In singing music without a clear tonic tone, the student must rely on a sure sense of interval. He must be able to recognize the size of any interval immediately, reduce complex-looking enharmonic intervals to simpler forms, and sing from tone to tone by interval. Occasionally a student may be able to translate groups of three or four tones as a known chordal pattern; for example, G♯-C-E♭, translated, is an A♭ triad.

Rhythms in Chapter 14

4   TENDREMENT   DAQUIN

5   ANDANTE   ROSSINI

6   LENTE   CHAMBONIERES

7   ANDANTE   DJARGOMISKY

8   ADAGIO   BACH

9   ALLEGRETTO, MARZIALE   ADAM

10   FEURIG   BRAHMS

11 ALLEGRETTO   VERDI

12 ANDANTE   SALIERI

13   ADAGIETTO   ROSSINI

14 ZART   MOZART

15   ANDANTE   BRUNEAU

16   LENT   BIZET

17   LENTO   LISZT

18   TRANQUILLO   CHARPENTIER

19   LARGO, MA NON TROPPO   RAMEAU

20   APPASSIONATA   SPAIN

21   ALLEGRO CON BRIO   CHOPIN

26   Moderato

Vaughn Williams

27

Ireland

28

Kodaly

29   UNITED STATES

30   SCOTLAND

31   BORODIN

32   UN PEU ALLANT   IBERT

33   PIERNE

34   UNITED STATES

35   BRITTEN

36   DOUCEMENT   MILHAUD

GLOSSARY OF TEMPO AND EXPRESSION TERMS

Abbandono, with abandon
Adagietto, somewhat slow
Adagio, very slow
Affettuoso, with feeling
Agitato, agitated
Aimable, good-naturedly
Alla, in the style of
Allegretto, moderately fast
Allegro, fast
Amoroso, lovingly
Andante, moderately slow
Andantino, somewhat faster than *andante*
Anfanglich, in original tempo
Animato, spirited
Anmut, with grace
A piacere, freely
Appassionata, impassioned
A tempo, in original tempo
Ausdruckvoll, expressive
Ben, well, very
Bewegt, agitated
Breit, broadly
Brio, brilliance
Calore, warmth
Cantabile, in a singing style
Caressant, caressingly
Cedez, yielding
Chaleur, warmth
Commodo, easy-going tempo
Con, with (used with other terms)
Deciso, decidedly
Dolce, soft, sweet
Dolente, sad
Einfach, simply
Elegiaco, elegaic
Energico, energetically
Espressivo, expressive
Etwas, somewhat (used with other terms)
Feierlich, solemn
Fervore, fervor
Frei, free
Fröhlich, happy
Gai, gay
Gefühl, feeling
Gemächlich, leisurely
Gesangvoll, in a singing style
Geschwind, quick
Giocoso, humorously
Giusto, strict
Grandioso, with pomp
Grave, solemn, slow
Grazioso, gracefully
Innig, fervent, heartfelt
Klagend, mournfully
Kraftig, strong
Langoureux, languishing
Langsam, slow
Largamente, in a broad style

Larghetto, slower than *andante*
Largo, very slow and broad
Lebendig, vivacious
Leggiero, light, airy
Leise, soft, gentle
Lento, slow
Lieblich, in a loving manner
Lusingando, soft, coaxing
Lustig, cheerful
Mächtig, powerful
Maestoso, majestic
Marcato, decisively
Marziale, in march style
Mässig, moderate
Mazurka, mazurka
Meno, less (used with other terms)
Minuetto, minuet tempo
Molto, much, very
Mosso, motion
Nicht, not (used with other terms)
Pesante, loud and heavy
Piacere, freely in tempo
Più, more (used with other terms)
Poco, a little (used with other terms)
Pomposo, pompously
Presto, fast
Primo, first
Quasi, in the manner of, about
Rallentando, slowing down
Rasch, fast
Religioso, in a religious style
Risoluto, firm, resolute
Sanft, gently
Scherzando, scherzoso, playfully
Schnell, fast, rapidly
Sehnsuchtvoll, full of longing
Semplice, simply
Sempre, always (used with other terms)
Singend, lyrically
Smorzando, dying away
Sospirando, sighing
Sostenuto, sustained
Spiritoso, spirited
Stark, strong
Suave, agreeable, sweet
Subito, suddenly
Tanto, much
Teneramente, tenderly
Tenuto, hold (a single note)
Tranquillo, quietly, peacefully
Träumerisch, dreamy
Triste, sadly
Troppo, too much
Vif, Vivace, Vivo, Vite, quick, lively
Vigoroso, vigorous
Wuchtig, weighty
Zart, gently, tenderly
Ziemlich, somewhat